# Understanding
# Christian Beliefs

D1520183

Books in the *Preparing for a Bahá'í/Christian Dialogue* series

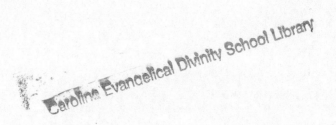
*Preparing for a*
*Bahá'í/Christian Dialogue*

Tahireh

VOLUME 2

# UNDERSTANDING
# CHRISTIAN BELIEFS

by

Michael W. Sours

ONEWORLD

OXFORD

Preparing for a Bahá'í/Christian Dialogue
Volume 2
Understanding Christian Beliefs

Oneworld Publications Ltd
185 Banbury Road, Oxford, OX2 7AR

A CIP record for this book is available from the British Library
ISBN  1-85168-032-2
Printed and bound in Great Britain

# contents

## Chapter 1

### INTRODUCTION TO CHRISTIAN DOCTRINES

## PART 1

### THE DIVINE INSPIRATION OF THE BIBLE

## Chapter 2

### THE AUTHORITY OF THE BIBLE

## Chapter 3

### THE AUTHENTICITY OF THE BIBLE

## Chapter 4

### RESPONDING TO CHRISTIAN OBJECTIONS

## PART 2

### THE DIVINITY OF CHRIST

## Chapter 5

### UNDERSTANDING THE RELATIONSHIP
### BETWEEN JESUS CHRIST AND GOD

*Chapter 6*

## RESPONDING TO CHRISTIAN
## ARGUMENTS ABOUT JESUS

*Chapter 7*

## THE PROPHETS AND THEIR CLAIM TO BE GOD

## PART 3

## THE SUBSTITUTIONARY ATONEMENT

*Chapter 8*

## THE MEANING OF ATONEMENT

*Chapter 9*

## THE MEANING OF SALVATION

*Chapter 10*

## RESPONDING TO CHRISTIAN
## ARGUMENTS ABOUT ATONEMENT

# PART 4

## THE RESURRECTION OF CHRIST

*Chapter 11*

## THE MEANING OF RESURRECTION

*Chapter 12*

## RESPONDING TO CHRISTIAN ARGUMENTS AGAINST THE SPIRITUAL INTERPRETATION OF THE RESURRECTION

## PART 5

*Chapter 13*

## CONCLUSION

*foreword*

## THE PURPOSE OF THIS BOOK

This is the second volume in a series of books intended to help Bahá'ís learn more about the Bible and present Bahá'u'lláh's teachings to Christians. Like Volume One it is intended for beginners and is written in a non-academic style. The previous volume focused on the importance of the Bible and methods of interpretation and on learning biblical evidence supporting the claims of Bahá'u'lláh. Now we will examine the relationship between some central Christian doctrines and Bahá'í teachings. Studying these doctrines and teachings will help us to answer many of the most common questions we are likely to encounter when discussing the Bahá'í Faith with Christians.

### The basic approach used in the *Preparing for a Bahá'í/Christian Dialogue* series

To help us present Bahá'u'lláh's message to Christians in a way that is both friendly and convincing, this volume, like its predecessor, takes two related and simple approaches, the first of which consists of the following basic steps:

- Emphasizing areas of agreement;

- Listening to other points of view and learning about the Scriptures, beliefs and terminology of those with whom we converse;

- Adapting our presentation to the particular terminology and temperament of the people to whom we speak.

Christians are generally more receptive to the Bahá'í Faith if we first remove their apprehensions about our beliefs. This is best accomplished by following the first step of emphasizing important areas of agreement. Our beliefs about Christ, the Bible and Christianity are all good subjects to begin with. For example, we can point out that the Bahá'í writings state that the divine origin of Christianity is 'unconditionally acknowledged, that the Sonship and Divinity of Jesus Christ are fearlessly asserted', and that 'the divine inspiration of the Gospel is fully recognized' (Shoghi Effendi, *Promised Day* 109). When shared beliefs are at the forefront of our discussions with Christians, it is naturally easier for them to perceive the true spirit of the Bahá'í Faith and be more receptive to the message of Bahá'u'lláh.

The courtesy of the second step can obtain similarly positive results. We should take the time to first listen and learn from others; such consideration and open-mindedness on our part will help us gain their respect. Listening to others, we will better inform ourselves of Christian beliefs and be better able to carry out the third step: adapting our presentations to the people to whom we speak. Knowledge of their particular terminology, temperament and questions will help us to speak their language and give the most appropriate answers. If we use terminology they are not familiar with, we may be misunderstood. The importance of listening to others cannot be stressed enough.

The second approach presented in Volume One was modelled after *The Book of Certitude (Kitáb-i-Íqán)*.[1] It also consists of three steps:

• Affirming the reliability of the Bible;

• Selecting appropriate criteria and evidence from the Bible; and then

1. See *Preparing for a Bahá'í/Christian Dialogue*, Volume 1, ch. 2.

• Using the biblical criteria and evidence to demonstrate the truth of Bahá'u'lláh's claims and teachings.

Obviously, these two approaches are mutually supportive of each other. The first stresses the need to emphasize important areas of agreement, while the second stresses the importance of always specifically emphasizing the Bahá'í acceptance of the Bible's divine inspiration and authority.

In reality, the three steps based on *The Book of Certitude* differ from the first approach only in that the Bible has become the focus, not the Christian believer. Thus, as well as listening to each individual Christian and learning about their personal beliefs and outlook, we should also be learning directly from the Bible. Moreover, the Bible itself becomes the primary source of terminology and evidence. We no longer merely adopt the terminology of a particular individual or group of Christians.

These approaches are not only about providing accurate answers to Christian questions. They are about attitude. They embody important Bahá'í beliefs about the recognition of other religions and such qualities as courtesy and goodwill. Putting these ideals into practice will help us to present our beliefs in accordance with Bahá'u'lláh's injunction: 'Consort with the followers of all religions in a spirit of friendliness and fellowship' (*Tablets of Bahá'u'lláh* 22).[2]

---

2. The views expressed in this volume, like those in Volume 1, reflect the research and opinions of this writer and do not represent an 'official Bahá'í view'.

$_c$ $^h$ $^a$ $^P$ $^t$ $^e$ $_r$

# 1

## INTRODUCTION
## TO CHRISTIAN DOCTRINES

### THE IMPORTANCE OF UNDERSTANDING CHRISTIAN DOCTRINES

Understanding Christianity requires both knowledge of the Bible and knowledge of the Christian view of what the Bible teaches. It is helpful to possess this knowledge in order to give answers appropriate to Christian questions.

Christian beliefs are expressed in 'doctrines'. The word originates from a Greek word that means 'teaching' or 'that which is taught' (see Matt. 7:28 and Rom. 16:17). Since early times Christian Churches have issued official statements and formal decrees stating, amending and sometimes changing the doctrines of Christianity. Ideally these doctrines are supposed to represent what the Bible actually teaches, but Christians have never fully agreed on all the relevant points. Disputes over doctrine have led to conflicts and to innumerable divisions within the Church. Doctrinal beliefs have changed throughout history and still vary among Christian denominations,[3] making it difficult to understand what Christians actually believe. Nevertheless, there are some points that can help us effectively sort things out. The first of these concerns the different types of modern Christian outlooks.

---

3. Basic information concerning the development of Christian doctrine can be found in many books. See, for example, A History of Christian Doctrines by Louis Berkhof.

## UNDERSTANDING SOME BASIC DIFFERENCES AMONG CHRISTIANS

In all ages various circumstances affect how people understand life and relate to one another. In recent centuries scientific discoveries have had an impact on beliefs about the Bible. Since the nineteenth century, scientific discoveries and the pressures from new trends and ideas - often termed by Christians 'modernism', or 'secular humanism' - have progressively led many people to question orthodox and traditional Christian beliefs. Many beliefs that rested more on tradition, nationalism and superstition than on the authority of the Bible have been rightly discarded. However, this process of challenging and rethinking traditional beliefs has also gradually undermined many basic Christian moral values and legitimate spiritual truths.[4] This is partly due to the misconception that when a new idea conflicts with a traditional literal interpretation of the Bible, it challenges the Bible and undermines religion itself, rather than merely challenges *how* the Bible has been traditionally interpreted and understood.

This conflict between modernism and traditional Christianity has led many to entirely reject Christianity. Others still adhering to Christianity are increasingly divided by a growing diversity of opinions about what the Bible actually teaches and about its authority. Christians conciliatory to modern trends are too 'liberal' for some, those holding to orthodox beliefs are too 'conservative' for

---

4. Shoghi Effendi refers to the 'menace of secularism' that has manifested 'itself in both Europe and America, and is, in varying degrees, and under various forms and designations, challenging the basis of every established religion, and in particular the institutions and communities identified with the Faith of Jesus Christ' (*World Order* 181). Moreover, he attributes the 'signs of moral downfall' to the 'decline of religion as a social force' and adds that when 'the light of religion is quenched in men's hearts', human character 'is debased, confidence is shaken, the nerves of discipline are relaxed, the voice of human conscience is stilled, the sense of decency and shame is obscured, conceptions of duty, of solidarity, of reciprocity and loyalty are distorted, and the very feeling of peacefulness, of joy and of hope is gradually extinguished' (*World Order* 186-7).

others. Today Christianity is commonly perceived to be divided into these two camps.[5]

Among the conservative Christians are those who ardently reassert what they believe are the traditional Christian beliefs and values. They sometimes refer to themselves as Evangelicals and/or Fundamentalists.[6] As well as upholding traditional values in their own lives, they believe they must fight against modern trends which they perceive to be undermining Christianity itself.[7]

When liberal influences have sometimes suggested the validity of other religions, some Fundamentalists have reacted by emphasizing Christianity as the only means to attain salvation.[8] When it became clear that modern theories of evolution had gained widespread acceptance over traditional literal interpretations of the Bible (especially the Book of Genesis), some Fundamentalists reacted with the elaborate theory of 'creationism'.[9] And, as people have begun to espouse the need for a world government, some Fundamentalists have argued against it, equating world

5. These distinctions are explained in William E. Hordern's book *A Layman's Guide to Protestant Theology*. Hordern also makes in his book the important observation that theological differences no longer follow clear denominational lines (257).
6. In *The World Order of Bahá'u'lláh*, Shoghi Effendi examines the forces affecting Christians in the modern era (179-86).
7. The Fundamentalist viewpoint, as well as some of the difficulties of defining who is a Fundamentalist or Evangelical, can be understood from reading the following books: George Marsden ed., *Evangelicalism and Modern America*, and Jerry Falwell ed., *The Fundamentalist Phenomenon*. Also, in *Fundamentalism and American Culture*, Marsden presents a historical overview that examines various factors influencing Fundamentalism in its American context and discusses why Fundamentalists became viewed by many as 'those who for sociological reasons held on to the past in stubborn and irrational resistance to inevitable changes in culture' (185).
8. See Josh McDowell and Don Stewart, *Understanding Non-Christian Religions*. Josh McDowell is a popular Christian apologist arguing for the conservative Christian point of view. McDowell is author of numerous books and frequently a lecturer on college campuses as a representative of the Campus Crusade for Christ.
9. 'The emphasis laid by the Protestant Reformers on the verbal inspiration of the Bible led to a more literal interpretation, and by the eighteenth century an acceptance of the details of the story of organic creation, as given in the first chapter of Genesis, became necessary to orthodoxy. In the nineteenth it was apparently believed by almost the whole Christian world. Geological study must have suggested doubts about the chronology of Archbishop Ussher, who put the date of creation in the year 4004 B.C., but even such a well-informed man as Philip Goss seriously contended in 1857 that God had put misleading fossils into rocks to test the faith of mankind.' (Sir William Dampier, *A History of Science and its Relation with Philosophy and Religion* 334). Today, views such as those of Goss can still be found among some Christians but the concept of

government with a literal interpretation of biblical prophecies about an antichrist.[10]

Every new development is followed by a new reaction. Rather than reconsider how the Bible should be interpreted and understood, Fundamentalists generally insist on the imitation of the views of the past. Liberal Christians, on the other hand, will sometimes relinquish select portions of the Bible with little hesitation. Thus, the 'cleavage between the fundamentalists and the liberals among their [i.e., various Christian denominations] adherents is continually widening'.[11]

The distinguishing feature of conservatives is their attitude towards the Bible, and especially their view that it should be interpreted literally. We must be aware of this because when the Bible is taken literally it not only conflicts with modern science, but also with other religions including the Bahá'í Faith. This is one of the reasons why the *Preparing for a Bahá'í/Christian Dialogue* series focuses specifically on how we can best discuss the Bahá'í teachings with conservative Christians. However, the tendency to interpret the Bible literally is also the dominant approach among Christians all over the world. The authority of the Bible and belief in a physical resurrection are, for example, still common to all major Christian denominations in North, Central and South America, Africa, the missionary field of Asia and among most active Christians in European countries and so on. All the controversies among liberal scholars over

creationism has become more common. For a concise presentation of creationism, see Arlie J. Hoover, *Fallacies of Evolution*. This book is principally an argument for teaching creationism in public schools. A more detailed explanation of creationism can be found in *Scientific Creationism* (Public School Edn), prepared by the Institute for Creation Research, Henry Morris ed. A rebuttal to creationism by Protestant, Catholic and Jewish theologians can be found in *Is God a Creationist?*, Roland Mushat Frye, ed. See also George M. Marsden's, *Fundamentalism and American Culture* 149. Marsden provides one of the lesser known and more interesting reasons for the reaction against evolution.
10. See, for example, Hal Lindsey's *The Late Great Planet Earth*, ch. 9, 'The Future Fuehrer.' Lindsey's interpretations have been discredited in most people's eyes by recent political changes.
11. Shoghi Effendi, *World Order* 183.

the Bible have not persuaded a single sizeable denomination to omit even one book from the Bible. By listening and asking questions, we can determine very quickly whether or not we are speaking with a liberal or conservative Christian. Nevertheless, we should keep in mind that these are very general categories and neither exists as an entirely consistent ideological group.

In an attempt to mend some of the divisions between Christians, and thus halt the decline of their influence, Fundamentalists have struggled to find a basis for some unity of thought among their conservative Christians allies. They have not sought unity through any concessions of belief but rather by building alliances through stressing what to them are the most important doctrines. It is these doctrines which we need to learn about most.

### FIVE MAIN DOCTRINES

Despite the differences that exist between Christians, there are certain doctrines that are more widely held and less disputed than others. In a 1981 publication, *The Fundamentalist Phenomenon* (edited by Jerry Falwell, a leading advocate of Fundamentalism in America) five traditional doctrines were asserted as basic to true Christianity. These doctrines were presented as the ground on which all Christians could and should take a united stand. The doctrines listed concerned: (1) the authority of Scripture, (2) the nature of Christ, (3) the substitutionary atonement, (4) the resurrection of Christ, and (5) the Second Advent.

Our concern will not be with assessing the nature of Fundamentalism, its fluctuating influence as a movement, or its struggle against modern trends, good and bad. In this volume we will simply be concerned with the first four of these particular doctrines which are broadly accepted among many Christians - including Catholics, Eastern Orthodox and most of the major divisions of Protestantism[12] - and with how they can affect Christian responses to the Bahá'í Faith. With each examination we will briefly consider a Christian point of view as well as a Bahá'í point of view. The fifth doctrine will be examined in Volume Three of this series.[13]

Studying these doctrines will help us learn ways to overcome some of the barriers preventing Christians from recognizing the truth of Bahá'u'lláh's claims. Since they assume that their doctrinal understanding accurately reflects the intended meaning of the Bible, some Christians have used these doctrines to argue that Christianity is the only possible means to salvation. Moreover, some have argued that Bahá'í beliefs are incompatible with biblical Christianity. These views can prevent Christians from seeing the validity of other religions and the claims of Bahá'u'lláh. It is possible to resolve these difficulties, but to do so it is of vital importance that we avoid controversial disputes which will undermine the 'spirit of friendliness and fellowship' (*Tablets of Bahá'u'lláh* 22).

---

12. With respect to the number of adherents, Christianity is the largest of the world's religions. Of Christians, the Roman Catholics constitute the largest Christian group, but it is the Protestants (particularly the conservative denominations) who are gaining the most new adherents. There are estimated to be over one hundred million people who in some way identify with Christianity in North American, over four hundred million in Latin America, and over one hundred million in the Soviet Union (even before the changes of 1989-90 in Eastern Europe and Russia). In Africa there are thought to be as many as two hundred million Christians and in East and South Asia nearly another two hundred million. The vast majority of the Christians in Africa and Asia are the result of missionary efforts undertaken in the last 150 years. The conservative Christians are especially notable in their missionary achievements. Of the major world religions - Christianity, Hinduism, Buddhism and Islam - it is the Christians who have, unquestionably, the world's most effective ongoing missionary programme. They have created written scripts for peoples who had none and taken literacy to the world's most remote regions in order to make the Bible available to everyone. All these efforts have helped the spread of a language of religious terminology, and an expression of messianic expectation that will, no doubt, make it all that much easier for people to understand and appreciate Bahá'u'lláh's Revelation once they encounter it.
13. It was originally intended that all five doctrines would be examined in this volume. However, since Volume Three is specifically concerned with the subject of prophecy it is more appropriate to examine the doctrine of the Second Coming in that volume.

## A KEY FOR UNDERSTANDING SCRIPTURE: A BRIEF INTRODUCTION TO BAHÁ'Í THEOLOGY

Bahá'u'lláh says that all the 'Divine Messengers have been sent down, and their Books were revealed, for the purpose of promoting the knowledge of God and furthering unity and fellowship amongst men' (*Epistle* 12). Knowledge of God and fellowship are corollaries. In the Bible it is stated that humankind is created in the image of God (Gen. 1:26; *Promulgation* 29, 69). This affirms that humankind has a spiritual nature and that this nature defines our purpose: to reflect the image of God. Accepting this as our purpose, we must acquire some knowledge of God in order to achieve it. For example, the realization that God is one indicates that we must also be one, that is, unified. This requires that we strive as best we can to reflect God's love, mercy, compassion and other divine attributes in our relations with all people, including the followers of other Faiths. Knowledge of God is thus directly linked to fellowship among ourselves and with non-Bahá'ís.

Since knowledge and fellowship are the underlying purpose of the revealed Books of God, any understanding of Scripture that fails to discover this knowledge or fails to be a source of fellowship misses the very purpose of Scripture. Scripture is a Revelation from God, that is, it reveals God, and if correctly understood, we will see in it the attributes of God. In all the doctrines examined in this book, an underlying difference can be seen between the Bahá'í and Christian understanding of the Bible, the deity of Christ, the atonement and the resurrection. This difference is the result of the Bahá'í application of the knowledge of God to the interpretation of Scripture. For example, some Christians assert that the Bible is the only and final Revelation from God. The Bahá'í Faith accepts that the Bible is the Word of God but rejects all interpretations asserting a finality to God's

Revelation on the grounds that such interpretations do not reflect God's all-encompassing grace and God's love for all humankind.[14] Similarly, the Bahá'í Faith accepts that Christ is the incarnation of all the names and attributes of God, but rejects the Christian interpretation of the Incarnation, which asserts that the essence of God took on the limitations of corporal existence, because it does not reflect God's transcendence (*World Order* 112, *Certitude* 98). With regard to atonement, 'Abdu'l-Bahá acknowledges the atoning power of Jesus' death, but strongly rejects the doctrine of original sin because it conflicts with God's justice (*Promulgation* 449). The Bahá'í Faith affirms the resurrection but rejects its traditional literal interpretation on the basis, again, of God's transcendence. Ascension to heaven, the realm of God, via the physical plane of existence, is impossible because God is not contained within the realm of material limitations (*Some Answered Questions*, ch. 23).

In all instances, the Bahá'í understanding and interpretation involves and reflects a fundamental understanding of God. This is helpful to keep in mind, for the interpretation of Scripture should primarily serve the purpose of gaining knowledge of God and fostering fellowship. By keeping the knowledge of God foremost in our minds, we will be better able to understand and interpret all aspects of the Scriptures, not only Christian doctrines. Studying the *Book of Certitude* is an especially effective way of gaining a better understanding of the relationship between Bahá'í theology and the interpretation of Scripture.

---

14. This concept of God's grace is stated repeatedly in the *The Book of Certitude* (e.g., 99ff) and is implied in the entire concept of Progressive Revelation. Bahá'u'lláh writes: 'Thou art surely aware of their idle contention, that all Revelation is ended, that the portals of Divine mercy are closed, that from the daysprings of eternal holiness no sun shall rise again, that the Ocean of everlasting bounty is forever stilled, and that out of the Tabernacle of ancient glory the Messengers of God have ceased to be made manifest . . . These people have imagined that the flow of God's all encompassing grace and plenteous mercies, the cessation of which no mind can contemplate, has been halted' (*Certitude* 137). Besides grace, the belief in the finality of Revelation also involves the contradiction of other divine attributes. See *Certitude* 135-6.

Although there are differences between Bahá'í and some Christian interpretations of the Bible, many important points are held in common, such as the acceptance that the Bible is the Word of God, that Jesus is the Christ and that following Christ and the Bible leads to eternal life. Whatever the differences of interpretation or understanding about what constitutes the knowledge of God, they should never be allowed to undermine the other underlying purpose of God's holy Books: fellowship. Having knowledge of God is not adequate if it is not reflected in how we live and interact with other people.

It is possible to have a correct intellectual understanding of God's attributes while inadequately reflecting God in our interactions with other people. It is also possible to have a mistaken understanding of God's attributes, but, through associating in a spirit of friendliness and fellowship, reveal a beautiful reflection of God in our lives. Obviously, learning to reflect the image of God is an ongoing struggle and a gradual process. The forces of prejudice and divisiveness are very powerful and they can easily pull us down. We must consciously emphasize not only the finding of the right answers to specific questions, but also the seeking of areas of mutual agreement in order to establish a spirit of friendliness and fellowship with Christians.

## AVOIDING COUNTER-PRODUCTIVE CONTROVERSIES

In order to avoid unnecessary disputes it is best only to mention controversial points of doctrines when asked, only when it is truly important and, above all, only after emphasizing the more important areas of agreement. Some doctrinal issues are frequently a source of heated disagreement even among Christians; this alone is sufficient justification for extreme caution. These disagreements can lead to antagonism, which is 'always destructive to the truth' ('Abdu'l-Bahá, *Promulgation* 72).

If we are not careful, we can become involved in long, fruitless discussions which end unresolved, leaving no opportunity even to discuss who Bahá'u'lláh is or the central teachings of the Bahá'í Faith. Shoghi Effendi provides this extremely important guidance:

> refrain, under any circumstances, from involving yourselves, much less the Cause, in lengthy discussions of a controversial character, as these besides being fruitless actually cause incalculable harm to the Faith. Bahá'u'lláh has repeatedly urged us not to engage in religious controversies, as the adepts of former religions have done. The Bahá'í teacher should be concerned above all in presenting the Message, in explaining and clarifying all its aspects rather than in attacking other religions. He should avoid all situations that he feels would lead to strife, to hairsplitting and interminable discussions. [15]

It is vital to keep in mind that when we have discussions with Christians, our objectives are to set forth the truth of Bahá'u'lláh. We should avoid pointing out and emphasizing what seem to be errors in Christian doctrine, and instead seek out aspects of their beliefs upon which we can build agreement. In this book we will learn that this is not difficult because there are many important points of agreement between each of the central Christian doctrines and the Bahá'í teachings. These points of agreement can become the means for building that essential foundation of respect and fellowship which should always be established

---

15. From a letter (dated 29 November 1937) written on behalf of Shoghi Effendi to an individual believer, *Individual and Teaching*, 24.

first ('Abdu'l-Bahá, *Promulgation* 72-3). The foremost cornerstone of this foundation is, with Christians, our unhesitating acceptance of 'the Divinity of Jesus Christ' and the full recognition of 'the divine inspiration of the Gospel' (Shoghi Effendi, *Promised Day* 109). Every additional point of agreement is an additional stone upon this foundation.

Once this foundation is established, it will be easier to discuss issues and investigate the truth. The resultant spirit of fellowship will provide opportunities for explaining the teachings of Bahá'u'lláh and the evidence establishing His truth. It will also make it easier to talk about, when necessary, those aspects of Christian doctrine where we disagree. But remember, frequently there is no need to discuss any points where differences exist. In fact, some Christians are even annoyed by such discussions, and especially discussion on the more obscure points of doctrine. If the Christian, or Christians, to whom we are speaking bring out points of disagreement that need to be addressed, then we can rely on the knowledge we have acquired in our study of the Bible and Bahá'í writings. This knowledge will enable us to respond by directly referring to the Bible to demonstrate its support for the Bahá'í view. This way our affirmation of the Bahá'í point of view is also in the context of, and supported by, an affirmation that the Bible is a legitimate and authoritative way of seeking out the truth.

Reliance on the Bible is vital to our approach, especially since many Christians regard the Bible as the ultimate authority for correctly defining Christian doctrines. This is so much the case that the authority of the Bible itself is central to the doctrines of most Christian Churches. Therefore we will begin our study by examining Christian and Bahá'í teachings concerning the Bible.

*part one*

## THE DIVINE INSPIRATION OF THE BIBLE

**INTRODUCTION**

The most important cornerstone in any successful dialogue with Christians is the Bahá'í acceptance of the Bible. For this reason it is especially important that we have a clear understanding of the subject. In Chapter 2, Christian and Bahá'í beliefs about the Bible's authority and inspiration are explained. In Chapter 3 we will study Bahá'í writings concerning the authenticity of the Bible. Then, in Chapter 4, we will learn how to respond to Christian arguments that the Bible is the only and last Book containing God's Word.

chapter

2

## THE AUTHORITY OF THE BIBLE

### CHRISTIAN BELIEFS ABOUT THE AUTHORITY OF THE BIBLE

In the course of Christian history, belief and conduct have been shaped by reason, the institution of the Church and the interpretation of the Bible itself. Among the doctrines of the Church there evolved some that actually had little or no support in the Bible. The addition of such beliefs and practices led to protest within the Church itself eventually developing into a major schism (division in the Church) known as the Protestant Reformation.[16]

When the Protestant movement broke away from the Roman Catholic Church in the sixteenth century, Protestants rejected the belief that the authority of the Church was sufficient justification for unbiblical teachings. They insisted that beliefs must be based upon the ultimate authority of the inspired words of Scripture. This emphasis on the Bible as a source of Christian faith has made the authority of the Bible a fundamental concern for Protestants, so that any assertion that the Bible is unreliable is often perceived as a challenge to its authority and, in turn, to beliefs based on it.

---

16. The Guardian points out that the sacraments, rites and ceremonies of the Church had not 'reposed on the direct authority of Christ, or emanated from His specific utterances'. He adds that eventually this led to voices being 'raised in protest against the self-appointed Authority which arrogated to itself privileges and powers which did not emanate from the clear text of the Gospel of Jesus Christ, and which constituted a grave departure from the spirit which that Gospel did inculcate. They argued with force and justification that the canons promulgated by the Councils of the Churches were not divinely-appointed laws, but were merely human devices which did not even rest upon the actual utterances of Jesus' (*World Order*, 20-1, see also *Lights of Guidance* 373).

Since the Bahá'í writings support the authority of the Bible this should not be a problem. However, the greatest difficulty occurs when there are differences of opinion about what constitutes an assertion that the Bible is unreliable. For example, in extreme cases acceptance of the theories of evolution or that the earth is older than 6,000 years is considered anti-biblical. Such attitudes, of course, account for much of the antagonism that has existed and still exists between very conservative Christians and the scientific community.

To help us better understand Christian views on the Bible it is helpful to study some of the terms conservative Protestants use when they discuss the Bible's authority.

## UNDERSTANDING CHRISTIAN TERMINOLOGY

Protestant beliefs about the Bible usually involve the following three terms: (1) divine inspiration, (2) infallibility, and (3) inerrancy. The definitions we will examine are based mainly on the clarifications found in Floyd Barackman's *Practical Christian Theology* and are typical[17]:

• **Divine Inspiration** This term pertains to the assertion that the Scriptures are the act of the Holy Spirit working through the human agent to convey orally the word of God. It should be noted that Christians apply the term inspiration with various meanings and to varying degrees. Some believe that certain portions of the Bible are more inspired than others, and that some parts may not be inspired at all. This belief is known as the Variable Inspiration Theory. Others believe God inspired the

---

17. Floyd H. Barackman is an evangelical Christian who is an instructor in systematic theology at the Practical Bible Training School, Bible School Park, New York. His book *Practical Christian Theology* is a good example of what is called 'systematic Christian theology'. Its strong literalist interpretations are in many instances the antithesis of the Bahá'í approach, nevertheless, within

original writers with concepts which He then allowed them to express according to their own particular capacities. This view is known as the Inspired Concept Theory. Another theory, the Dictation Inspiration Theory, asserts that God dictated every word of the original writings.

These are some of the principal theories. There are others, and many Christians also combine certain ideas with more than one theory. Perhaps the theory that has gained the widest acceptance today is the Plenary-Verbal Inspiration Theory. This view holds that the Spirit of God protected the writers from errors while allowing them to freely express their own personalities and individual literary talents.

- **Infallibility** This term pertains to the assertion that the intrinsic teachings and doctrines of the Scriptures are true and reliable. Barackman makes the important distinction that this truth relates to what the Scriptures actually teach rather than to what people think the Scriptures teach.

- **Inerrancy** This term pertains to the assertion that the Scriptures are free of all errors, not only involving teachings but also the recording of facts, historical or otherwise. This view, like the ones mentioned above, is usually asserted only with regard to the original documents.

A less common definition of inerrancy is simply that the original authors of the Bible did not mean anything that could be construed as an error.

conservative Christian thought, this book gained the recommendation of such Christian leaders as: Dr John F. Walvoord, President, Dallas Theological Seminary; Joseph Y. Wong, Th.D, Academic Vice-President, Multnomah School of the Bible; and Dr H.L. Willmington, Vice President, Liberty Baptist College.

## CONTROVERSIES IN CHRISTIAN TERMINOLOGY

Christians may want to know whether or not, or to what degree, the Bahá'í Faith accepts these terms and definitions with regard to the Bible. That Christians are not in agreement over these issues is not something we need to point out to them, but we should bear in mind that their questioning of our position on the authority of the Bible may be to determine on which side of the controversy we stand. Our objective is not to take sides and become another voice in such disputes.[18]

The debate among Christians primarily centres on the extent to which these three terms are applicable to the Bible, particularly the concept of inerrancy. It is a very widely held belief that the Scriptures are the Word of God and contain infallible teachings. Any errors that might be found in the text are not believed to be significant enough to diminish either the reality of the Scriptures as the Word of God or the infallibility of the teachings that the Scriptures express. However, beyond such a general conviction, the application of the term inerrancy is strongly debated. Some maintain that only the original utterances and writings can be considered inerrant. These originals no longer exist. Others believe that virtually every last word in modern editions is still inerrant.[19]

Christians who maintain that only the original utterances and writings can be considered inerrant usually back

18. The following books specifically deal with the differences of belief about the Bible that exist among Christians: *The Battle for the Bible*, by Harold Lindsell; *The Bible in the Balance*, also by Lindsell; and *The Authority and Interpretation of the Bible*, by Jack B. Rogers and Donald K. McKim. The two books by Lindsell express and argue for the very conservative viewpoint. Lindsell's second book was written to strengthen his arguments in his first book by answering the criticisms it received. Both books have been very popular. Jack B. Rogers' and Donald K. McKim's book offers a broad historical overview of Christian beliefs about the Bible and challenges the argument that the conservative evangelical view represents the view historically held by the Church.
19. Even in recent times some Christian writers such as Halley made statements that suggest God dictated the Books of the Bible Himself. See Henry H. Halley, *Halley's Bible Handbook* 23. Very few Christian theologians and scholars hold such views today.

themselves up with reference to the errors in recent or known editions of the Bible. For instance, Barackman states that in the *King James Version*, Song of Solomon, 'he' had been mistranslated as 'she' (2:7, 3:5, 8:4).[20] Other similar errors in earlier manuscripts of the Bible are believed to have entered the text when the Scriptures were transcribed or translated. Any fair-minded person will acknowledge that these errors are real but have not been significant enough to cause distortions of doctrine or to affect the reliability of the Bible as a basis for faith, guidance and moral conduct. But the factual existence of such errors, although of minor significance, does mean that complete inerrancy can refer only to God's Word and not to the work of humans who translate, transcribe, print or interpret it.

Having knowledge of the type of errors that Christians such as Barackman have pointed out, and even being able to locate the documentary evidence to back it up is not necessarily, however, of much use or benefit in discussions with Christians. The authority of the Bible is a sensitive issue of utmost importance to many conservative Christians and any attempt to argue too forcefully against it will antagonize them. Our goal should be to avoid controversy by emphasizing a reliance on the Bible, without accepting or rejecting non-biblical terminology and non-biblical definitions of terminology such as 'inerrancy'. We should also demonstrate the Bahá'í view by simply basing what we say on what the Bible and Bahá'í writings actually say. As we will see, this is a very safe and effective approach to take.

## THE CLAIM OF INSPIRATION
Unlike the terms 'infallibility' and 'inerrancy', the term

---

20. A few other such minor errors can be found listed in Barackman's *Practical Christian Theology* 423. Most books documenting the history of the Bible include some examples, but scholars differ widely as to what constitutes an error in, or an addition to, the texts. See footnote 33.

'inspiration' is found in the New Testament with specific reference to Scripture. Paul writes:

> All Scripture is given by inspiration of God, and is profitable for doctrine, for reproof, for correction, for instruction in righteousness, that the man of God may be complete, thoroughly equipped for every good work. (2 Tim. 3:16-17)

This statement implies a criterion for determining what constitutes Scripture. Scripture is that which is 'given by inspiration of God' and we can determine this by whether or not such writings are 'profitable for doctrine, for reproof, for correction, for instruction in righteousness'. All of these points emphasize the spiritual goal of enabling 'the man of God' to be 'complete'.

These points are important because determinants of true Scripture do not rest on isolated and unspecific endorsements such as this by Paul, but rather on the actual spiritual qualities and authority evident in the words. Bahá'u'lláh Himself, with specific reference to the Bible, writes: 'Reflect: the words of the verses themselves testify to the truth that they are of God'. (*Certitude* 84)

The ability to recognize the inherent spiritual quality and authority of Scripture is important because Paul's statement does not identify which books should be considered genuine. That is, Paul states, 'all Scripture is given by inspiration of God', but neither he nor Christ, nor the other Apostles list which existing Books, Epistles, letters or other writings, Old Testament or New Testament, should specifically comprise 'all Scripture'. Therefore, the early Church leaders had to gather together the existing new documents and those thought to be inspired by the ministry of Christ and attributed to the Apostles, and determine which ones should be regarded as part of the canon (that is, a list of books officially accepted as genuine). However, even to this day, there are some disputes about the canonicity of a few books.[21]

It should be understood that the basic contents of the Bible were not determined by a list drawn up by either Christ or the Apostles; rather, it was dependent on the later recognition of the merits of the Books themselves. However, the reason for briefly mentioning these points is not to cast any doubt on the selection of the sacred Books now comprising the Bible. In fact, from a Bahá'í point of view, the statements found in the Qur'án, the Bahá'í writings and the records of 'Abdu'l-Bahá's talks provide the most direct, authoritative and complete affirmations of the existing Bible. The specific references to the Gospel, for example, affirming that the Christians have, and have had, the guidance of 'genuine texts' (*Certitude* 89) and that these are divinely inspired (*Promised Day* 109), provide an assurance entirely independent of that given by any Church authority.

However, in addition to such positive statements in the Bahá'í writings, we can affirm that the 'Scripture is given by the inspiration of God' (2 Tim. 3:16-17) by coming to know for ourselves its divine guidance, how it 'kindleth the love of God', enshrines 'the mysteries of an inscrutable wisdom', bestows 'wealth without gold', and confers 'immortality without death' (*Certitude* 198). These spiritual qualities are powerful evidences of divine inspiration that we can experience for ourselves.

---

21. Most notably, some pre-Christian books are included in the Bibles of the Roman Catholic, Eastern Orthodox and Coptic Churches, but excluded from Protestant editions. These books are called the 'Apocrypha' by Protestants, but in Roman Catholic usage are referred to as 'deuterocanonical'. It is generally, though not universally, acknowledged that the acceptance or rejection of these particular books has no appreciable effect on Christian doctrine. A presentation of the Protestant view of these and other disputed books can be found in many books about the history of the Bible. See, e.g., Norman L. Geisler's *A General Introduction to the Bible*.

The meaning of divine inspiration is that it breathes eternal life or the life of faith into us. As we have seen, Paul states that all Scripture is given by the 'inspiration' of God. The original Greek word is 'theopneustos' meaning 'God-breathed' (*Theos* is Greek for 'God', *pneo* means 'to breathe')[22]. 'Abdu'l-Bahá, uses similar terminology in one of His discourses explaining how Christ fulfilled the prophecies of the Old Testament. He stated, 'The Spirit breathing through the Holy Scriptures is food for all who hunger' (*Paris Talks* 57).

It therefore seems entirely appropriate to acknowledge with Christians that the Bible is inspired of God.[23] We can know this by accepting the testimony found in the Bible, the Bahá'í writings and the record of 'Abdu'l-Bahá's talks, and/or by directly experiencing this divine inspiration for ourselves.

## THE CLAIM OF INFALLIBILITY

The term 'infallibility' is not used in the Bible, but, since God's 'words are not false' (Job 36:4-5), God is 'perfect in

22. See Vine's *Expository Dictionary of Biblical Words* 328.
23. The word *Pentateuch* is from the Greek *penta*, meaning five, and is used to indicate the first five Books of the Bible which are traditionally attributed to the authorship of Moses, as is also suggested by the *Book of Certitude* (p. 199). This does not mean, however, that Moses actually wrote these Books in the form that we have them, any more than Jesus wrote the four Gospels. The four Gospels are traditionally believed to have been written by the Apostles, but because Jesus is the source of their inspiration they are, so to speak, Jesus' 'Book'. Similarly, while the authorship of the Pentateuch remains unclear, the five Books are regarded as inspired, independent of whether they were inspired by His original teachings or are basically descendants of His actual writings. The question of authorship should not be taken to mean that these Books are unreliable or uninspired. In the Gospel, the Qur'án and the Bahá'í sacred writings there are clear testimonies affirming the Torah in general and many portions of all five books (the Pentateuch) in particular. In the original Persian texts of the *Book of Certitude* the word translated by the Guardian as 'Pentateuch' is 'Torat', from the Hebrew 'Torah'. This term means 'the Teaching' and has been translated at times in editions of the Bible as 'the Law'.

In Jewish belief the Torah is twofold. There is the written Torah and the oral Torah. Both are regarded by some Jews as the Revelation given to Moses by God (see, e.g., *Scriptures of the Oral Torah* 1ff). The written Torah is the Pentateuch and the oral Torah (which in time also came into written form) is the work of Jewish commentators. The oral Torah includes a collection of writings referred to as the Talmud. 'Abdu'l-Bahá rejects the authority of the Talmud (*Promulgation* 161). Also, in an untranslated Tablet (*Ma'idiy-i-Asmani*, Part II. 216-17), 'Abdu'l-Bahá appears to define the meaning of Torah as being only that which was revealed by Moses (presumably the Pentateuch) and rejects that the writings of the commentators or historians (presumably the Talmud) form a part of the true 'Torah'. In specific knowledge' (Job 37:16) and God's 'understanding is infinite' (Ps. 147:5), it is rightly understood that God, from the testimony of Scripture and the evidences of His works, is infallible. If God is infallible, it is logical to assume that His teachings are too.

As we have seen, respected conservative Christians generally apply this term only to the Bible's 'intrinsic teachings', that is, to what it 'actually' teaches and not necessarily to what we 'think' it teaches (*Practical Christian Theology* 422). In other words, the assertion that Scripture is infallible does not apply to the individual believer's interpretation of Scripture, or to the translation or transcription of the text.

In Bahá'u'lláh's teachings it is stated that the Messengers of God are infallible (*Tablets of Bahá'u'lláh* 108), that from their 'knowledge, the knowledge of God is revealed', and that they 'faithfully reflect the light of God' (*Certitude* 142). Thus we can expect to find the teachings of Moses and Christ, recorded in the Bible, to be reliable witnesses of the truth of God and His teachings.

---

'Abdu'l-Bahá rejects the narratives about the sins and transgressions of Lot and the other Prophets which He says were written by Jewish historians after Moses. It is, in fact, well known that much of the Talmud was not even written down until after Christ. The biblical account of Lot and certain incidents concerning Abraham and Moses have been traditionally interpreted by Jews and Christians to indicate sins on the part of these Prophets. In authoritative Bahá'í writings, each of these instances is referred to and these interpretations are rejected without ever rejecting the actual accounts in the Pentateuch.

This suggests that 'Abdu'l-Bahá's rejection of certain narratives contained in the 'Torat' may be a reference to the oral 'Torat' which was written by Jewish commentators and historians. Otherwise, if 'Abdu'l-Bahá is referring to the narratives in the Pentateuch, He may be intending that they are not 'wholly' reliable in every detail or in a strict historical sense, inasmuch as they are not the actual written documents of Moses but are in part the composition of later Jewish historians. If this is the case, it should be kept in mind that most of the main narratives of the Pentateuch are referred to in the Qur'án and Bahá'í sacred writings, such as the story of Adam and Eve, Noah, Lot, Abraham, Jacob, Joseph, the captivity of the Jews in Egypt and the Revelation of the Ten Commandments, all of which are cited for the benefit of our own spiritual instruction and in many cases with a prophetic connection to the Bahá'í Faith. Furthermore, in *Secret of Divine Civilization* 'Abdu'l-Bahá refers to the Pentateuch in support of an argument concerning what Abraham did not teach saying, 'In any case, the Pentateuch is *extant and available today*, and contains the laws of Abraham. Let them refer to it' (p. 29, emphasis added). The word translated here as *Pentateuch* is also Torat (Torah) and, in this case, the portion of the Torah that 'Abdu'l-Bahá is referring to forms part of the Book of Genesis. This is a further confirmation that what He means by 'Torah' is the first five books (i.e., the Pentateuch).

Moreover, the word 'infallible' also appears in Bahá'u'lláh's writings in connection with the Bible. In *The Book of Certitude*, Bahá'u'lláh speaks of the importance of attaining to the City of God. This City, He writes, is 'none other than the Word of God revealed in every age and dispensation. In the days of Moses it was the Pentateuch; in the days of Jesus the Gospel' (*Certitude* 199). In the course of His presentation, Bahá'u'lláh writes of the greatness of that City which is the Word of God. At one point He says that in that City we can 'hearken unto infallible proofs from the Hyacinth of that assembly and receive the surest testimonies' (ibid. 199). Here again, we must understand the distinction: this infallibility, as indicated in the Bible and the Bahá'í writings, does not pertain to the human interpretation, translation, or transcription of the text.

Nevertheless, Bahá'u'lláh does not indicate that errors in translation and transcription are so significant as to blot out the light of God from the texts, and hence excuse our inability to 'hearken unto infallible proofs'. With specific reference to the Gospel, in view of Bahá'u'lláh's argument that the Gospel has been protected by a 'gracious and loving Providence' (*Certitude* 89), it seems safe to assume that the intrinsic teachings of the original texts are intact. He says that a gracious and loving Providence protected the Gospel and assured the Christians of guidance until the advent of the Qur'án. In light of all the tangible evidence confirming that the Gospel has not undergone any significant corruption since the time of Muhammad, we are therefore forced to admit that the same 'text' that Bahá'u'lláh refers to as the 'heavenly Gospel' (*Certitude* 89) still exists today and is virtually free from any significant errors that might affect its intrinsic spiritual message or original guidance.[24]

---

24. There are many existing documents that pre-date Muhammad and which support the integrity of present editions of the Bible. See E.S. Buchanan, *The Records Unrolled*; Jack Finegan, *Encountering New Testament Manuscripts*; Sir Frederic Kenyon, *Our Bible and the Ancient Manuscripts*, or other books about the early textual evidence of the Bible.

Even though we regard Jesus as an infallible Manifestation of God, we must also make a distinction between Him and the Apostles. Bahá'u'lláh says:

> the term 'Infallibility' hath numerous meanings and divers stations. In one sense it is applicable to the One Whom God hath made immune from error. Similarly it is applied to every soul whom God hath guarded against sin, transgression, rebellion, impiety, disbelief and the like. (*Tablets of Bahá'u'lláh* 108)

Bahá'u'lláh then refers to one type of infallibility, designated as the 'Most Great Infallibility' (*Tablets of Bahá'u'lláh* 108), which can only be applied to the Manifestation of God; to the station of Jesus Christ, but not the station of the Apostles, who sometimes erred.

This, however, does not mean that we should separate Jesus' words from those of the Apostles, and call one inspired and the other not. Some editions of the Bible contain Jesus' words printed in red to help the reader distinguish them more clearly and follow the sequence of the dialogues more easily. This can be helpful and, obviously, the words attributed to Jesus deserve special reverence, but we must remember that the Gospel comes to us in the form of a narrative. It not only records some of the sayings of Jesus but also recounts the life of Jesus, who was 'the Word' (John 1:14, *Selections from the Writings of 'Abdu'l-Bahá* 60; *Promulgation* 154-5, 212, 409). Therefore, many of the passages that are not 'in red' are inspired by God inasmuch as they convey to us the perfect example of Christ's life.

Such inspiration is also seen in the interaction between the Apostles and Christ's message. For example, Jesus called Peter to be an Apostle of Christ (Matt. 4:18,19) and said Peter's recognition of Jesus' true station had been 'revealed' to

him by His 'Father who is in heaven' (Matt. 16:13-17). So
great was the station of Peter (whose name means a type of
rock) that Jesus said to him, 'you are Peter, and on this rock I
will build My church, and the gates of Hades [hell] shall not
prevail against it [the Church]'.[25] Moreover, Jesus gave
authority to Peter with these words, 'I will give you the keys
of the kingdom of heaven, and whatever you bind on earth
will be bound in heaven, and whatever you loose on earth
will be loosed in heaven' (Matt. 16:18-19).

Nevertheless, despite Peter's high station and authority,
he later denied that he knew Jesus in order to protect his own
safety, as is recorded in the accounts of the Gospel (e.g., Matt.
26:69-75; see also Matt. 26:31-5). Obviously, the words of
Peter's denial were not divinely inspired nor was this an
infallible act. However, the New Testament account of this
event is inspired in that it reveals God's transforming power.
Peter did not let his failure defeat him; instead he went on to
preach the Gospel of Christ, as is recorded in the Book of
Acts, and, according to tradition, he later gave his life as a
martyr.[26]

The Scriptures also record the un-inspired words and evil
deeds of those who opposed the Word of God. For example,
there were those who falsely accused Jesus, saying, 'He casts
out demons by the ruler of the demons' (see Matt. 9:33-4,
12:24). There is also the record of Herod who beheaded John
the Baptist, (Matt. 14:5-11) and so on. Bahá'u'lláh writes:

> The people living in the days of the Manifestations
> of God have, for the most part, uttered such
> unseemly sayings. These have been set down
> circumstantially in the revealed Books and Holy
> Scriptures. (*Gleanings* 189)

25. The Guardian acknowledges these statements as a legitimate substantiation for the 'primacy
of Peter'. (See *Lights of Guidance* 373; *Promised Day* 109.)
26. See *The Anti-Nicene Fathers*, vol. VII, 302.

Although the evil deeds and words of those who opposed the Prophets should never be confused with the inspired sayings of the Prophets, Christ or the Apostles, there are important reasons why they 'have been set down circum- stantially in the revealed Books and Holy Scriptures'. Bahá'u'lláh writes:

> Examine the wondrous behavior of the Prophets, and recall the defamations and denials uttered by the children of negation and falsehood, perchance you may cause the bird of the human heart to wing its flight away from the abodes of heedlessness and doubt unto the nest of faith and certainty. (*Certitude* 5-6)

He adds:

> the more closely you observe the denials of those who have opposed the Manifestations of the divine attribute, the firmer will be your faith in the Cause of God. (Ibid. 6)

These passages suggest the importance of viewing the sacred narratives as a whole, because the story of both the Prophets and Apostles and their opposers combine to form a message which is inspired and which can lead us to 'faith and certainty'(*Certitude* 6).

This leaves the question of how to regard the sayings of the Apostles in their epistles or letters, which are separate from the four versions of the Gospel. These Epistles contain only a few sayings attributable to Jesus, or recountings of His ministry. In considering this question it is worth noting the testimony of the Apostles themselves.

John, for example, writes, 'this is the message which we have heard from Him and declared to you' (1 John 1:5).

Similarly, Paul says, 'I have fully preached the gospel of Christ' (Rom. 15:19). Paul's general message, which forms the larger number of the Epistles, is affirmed by these words of Peter who states, 'the longsuffering of our Lord is salvation - as also our beloved brother Paul, according to the wisdom given to him, has written to you' (2 Pet. 3:15).

'Abdu'l-Bahá, moreover, indicates that Christ 'was the essence of the Word Itself' and the Apostles were 'as Letters' whose meaning was 'consonant with the Word' (*Selections from the Writings of 'Abdu'l-Bahá* 60).[27] Even though we do not accord the Apostles the same station of infallibility as that accorded to the Manifestations of God, their station is very exalted nonetheless and their efforts to faithfully convey the inspiration they received from the divine Person of Jesus should not be undervalued.

We must not fail to recognize the 'God-given authority' (*Promised Day* 107) of Books attributed to the Apostles and inspired by Jesus, since these Books were the ones that were left as guidance after Jesus' ascension. These accounts must, therefore, be generally regarded as Jesus' own 'Book'.

## THE CLAIM OF INERRANCY

As mentioned before, inerrancy is the most controversial term used with reference to the Bible's authority. Some Christians will argue that since God is perfect, God's Word is therefore without error and since the Bible is God's Word, then it must be without error. This argument is reasonable, but it is sometimes used to imply that a particular edition of

---

27. This point is discussed in Volume One of *Preparing for a Bahá'í/Christian Dialogue: Understanding Biblical Evidence.* Anyone who doubts the inspiration reflected in the words of the Apostles should carefully examine 'Abdu'l-Bahá's interpretations of, and attitude towards, the writings of the New Testament. See, for example, 'Abdu'l-Bahá's comments on John 1:1, of which He said, 'This is a brief statement but replete with the greatest meanings. Its applications are illimitable and beyond the power of books or words to contain and express' (*Promulgation* 154). Similarly, see 'Abdu'l-Bahá's commentary on Paul's statements about life through Christ (*Some Answered Questions*, ch. 24) or on Paul's interpretation of Mosaic Law and the need for the outward form of the Law to be abrogated (ibid. ch. 20).

the Bible must be without error and certain interpretations likewise. Such a view could lead to a number of extreme conclusions already rejected by many Christians themselves.

All considerations of terms such as inspiration, infallibility and inerrancy must be balanced against the fact that variations and transcription errors do exist in many of the earliest surviving documents of the Bible. If we become dogmatic or legalistic about theories concerning inerrancy we run the risk of falling into the fallacious over-generalization that if an error can be found in the transcription of even a small part of the Bible, the Bible as a whole is unreliable and/or the rest of the Bible is not God's Word.

Therefore it can be asserted, as already stressed, that God's Word does not contain errors but human transcription and interpretation do occasionally lead to some errors, even though very minor. In other words, early surviving records show clear evidence that there is a distinction between God's infallible Word and the sometimes detrimental effects fallible humans have had on that Word.

Christians who place emphasis on the issue of inerrancy usually do so for a reason. They are anxious to counter accusations that unjustly undermine the Bible's authority. Rather than take a position on this controversial issue, it is probably wiser to simply go to the heart of the matter. That is, assure them of the fact that the Bahá'í writings clearly state that we have no desire or intention of undermining the God-given authority of their Books (*Promised Day* 107).

In many cases, it is often best to provide Christians with information from the Bahá'í writings and let them draw their own conclusions. For example, we can point out that the Bahá'í writings frequently refer to the Bible, citing verses to explain spiritual truths or doctrines, to point out historical evidence and to enumerate prophecies concerning Christ, Muhammad, the Báb and Bahá'u'lláh. Such instances clearly suggest that, regardless of theories about inerrancy, the authority of the Bible is affirmed.

Nowhere in the authoritative Bahá'í writings, to this writer's knowledge, is there any assertion that doctrinal misunderstandings, immorality or failure to recognize a true prophet of God occurred because of mistakes in the text of the Bible. This is an  important point for us to keep in mind when discussing spiritual truths with Christians. We should not confuse misinterpretations of Scripture to mean there are mistakes of substance in the actual text.

In *The Book of Certitude* (p. 88), Bahá'u'lláh points out that when some Muslims were confronted by 'the claims advanced by Christians and the peoples of other faiths', the Muslims, 'knowing not what answer to give', tried to discount the authority of the Bible by making the false accusation, ' "These Books have been corrupted and are not, and never have been, of God" '.  Later, Bahá'u'lláh, while expounding on the same theme, rejects the assertions of these Muslims as 'utter falsehood and sheer calumny' (ibid.). When we are confronted by the claims of Christians we should not make the same mistake.

The affirmations of the Bible found in the Bahá'í writings are completely sufficient for our guidance and the best examples to follow in our approach to the Bible and Christians.  Following them will help us avoid fruitless hairsplitting over terminology.

Sometimes it is simply best to hear out the concerns of the Christians to whom we are speaking, then re-focus the question on other aspects of the truth that are more constructive and more spiritually conducive to fellowship and friendliness.  For example, questions concerning the extent of the Bible's infallibility or inerrancy are probably beyond our ability to fully determine or know, but we do know that the Bible can guide the believer to eternal life.

Moreover, we also believe it offers a confirmation of the truth of Bahá'u'lláh.

## THE RELATIVITY OF RELIGIOUS TRUTH

Whatever the greatness of the Bible we should keep in mind that this greatness does not diminish the importance of accepting Bahá'u'lláh, even as acceptance of the Old Testament does not remove the need to accept the truth of Christ and the New Testament. This is true for many reasons, one of which is the relativity and progressive nature of religious truth.

Some truths are eternal, such as the sovereignty of God and His love for us, and the way we understand these truths is relative to our own spiritual growth, rational capacities and human limitations. Consequently, because of the changing circumstances in the history of humankind, religious truth has, as the Bible itself indicates, been revealed progressively through the ages by different Prophets and in accordance with changing human needs. From a Bahá'í point of view this is true of all religions including those not belonging to the Western religious tradition. Understood from this point of view, and keeping in mind our human limitations, we must acknowledge, as Shoghi Effendi points out, that 'religious truth is not absolute but relative, that Divine Revelation is orderly, continuous and progressive and not spasmodic or final' (*World Order* 115) .

Understanding the relativity of religious truth is very important when we think about the authority of Scripture. Referring to the different religions of the world, Bahá'u'lláh writes:

> These principles and laws, these firmly-established and mighty systems, have proceeded from one Source, and are rays of one Light. That they differ one from

another is to be attributed to the varying requirements of the ages in which they were promulgated. (*Epistle* 13)

What is required in one age or place is, therefore, not necessarily required in another. For example, in the Old Testament there are many laws that were no longer applicable or needed in the time of Christ. 'Abdu'l-Bahá discusses the following instance:

> After Christ four disciples, among whom were Peter and Paul, permitted the use of animal food forbidden by the Bible, except the eating of those animals which had been strangled, or which were sacrificed to idols, and of blood [Acts 15:20]. They also forbade fornication. They maintained these four commandments. Afterward, Paul permitted even the eating of strangled animals, those sacrificed to idols, and blood, and only maintained the prohibition of fornication. So in chapter 14, verse 14 of his Epistle to the Romans, Paul writes: 'I know, and am persuaded by the Lord Jesus, that there is nothing unclean of itself: but to him that esteemeth any thing to be unclean, to him it is unclean'.
>    Also in the Epistle of Paul to Titus, chapter 1, verse 15: 'Unto the pure all things are pure: but unto them that are defiled and unbelieving is nothing pure; but even their mind and conscience is defiled.'
>    Now this change, these alterations and this abrogation are due to the impossibility of comparing the time of Christ with that of Moses. The conditions and requirements in the later period were entirely changed and altered. The former laws were, therefore, abrogated. (*Some Answered Questions*, ch. 20)

'Abdu'l-Bahá's words point out that the Old Testament laws were no longer suited to the needs of the believers and, therefore, the Apostles rightly used their authority to abrogate them. Another example can be found in the Bible's teachings regarding women. Paul perpetuates the Jewish law with these words, 'Let your women keep silent in the churches, for they are not permitted to speak; but they are to be submissive, as the law also says. And if they want to learn something, let them ask their own husbands at home' (1 Cor. 14:34-5). Hundreds of years later with the advent of the Islamic age, the Qur'án confirmed and re-established a similar type of male-dominated hierarchy. However in our age, the Bahá'í Dispensation, this teaching is in no way suitable and has been rightly changed. In one of His talks, 'Abdu'l-Bahá stated that Bahá'u'lláh 'establishes the equality of man and women. This is peculiar to the teachings of Bahá'u'lláh, for all other religions have placed man above women' (*Promulgation* 455). In another talk He states that Bahá'u'lláh has revealed that 'women must be given the privilege of equal education with man and full right to his prerogatives. That is to say, there must be no difference in the education of male and female in order that womankind may develop equal capacity and importance with man in the social and economic equation. Then the world will attain unity and harmony' (ibid. 108).

From these points we can understand that even though the Bible is the Word of God, not all of the laws or social teachings are applicable to our age. This has become so apparent that many Christians have themselves abandoned some New Testament teachings such as those regarding women.

## POINTS OF AGREEMENT: RESPECT FOR THE BIBLE IN THE BAHÁ'Í WRITINGS

As we have seen, there are some very strong points of agreement between the Christian and Bahá'í views concerning the divine inspiration of the Bible. These similarities of belief form one of the most immediate foundations for positive interaction between Christians and Bahá'ís. Therefore, it will be advantageous to take another brief, but closer, look at this important tenet of the Bahá'í Faith.[28]

Christians will sometimes imply, as has been this writer's personal experience, that Bahá'ís accept Bahá'u'lláh because of a lack of knowledge of the Bible, or that anyone who is a Bahá'í denies the validity of the Bible. These false assumptions need to be dispelled if we are going to be successful in conveying the truth of Bahá'u'lláh. This can be greatly facilitated by referring to the many passages in the Bahá'í writings defending, upholding and glorifying the Bible.

'Abdu'l-Bahá refers to the Bible as the 'Holy Bible' (*Promulgation* 198-9), the 'Holy Book' (*Tablets of Abdul-Baha Abbas* 218), and states that people 'fail to understand its priceless beauty' (*Paris Talks* 48). He urges Bahá'ís to 'know the value of the Bible' (*Tablets of Abdul-Baha Abbas* 218) and says, 'I beg of God through the confirmation and assistance of the True One thou mayest show the utmost eloquence, fluency, ability and skill in teaching the real significances of the Bible' (ibid. 243). And again, He says, 'Look at the Gospel of the Lord Christ and see how glorious it is!' (*Paris Talks* 48) and, 'You must follow the example and footprints of Jesus Christ. Read the Gospels' (*Promulgation* 42). 'Abdu'l-Bahá related to an audience in America that Bahá'u'lláh promoted the Bible in Persia:

Fifty years ago no one would touch the Christian Bible in Persia. Bahá'u'lláh came and asked, 'Why?' They said, 'It is not the Word of God.' He said, 'You must read it with understanding of its meanings, not

28. This topic was also briefly discussed in Volume One of *Preparing for a Bahá'í/Christian Dialogue: Understanding Biblical Evidence.*

as those who merely recite its words.' Now Bahá'ís
all over the East read the Bible and understand its
spiritual teaching. Bahá'u'lláh spread the Cause of
Christ and opened the book of the Christians and
Jews. (*Promulgation* 212)

Moreover, concerning the influence of the Bible, 'Abdu'l-
Bahá writes:

the New and Old Testaments propounded throughout
all regions the Cause of Christ and were the pulsating
power in the body of the world. (*Selections from the
Writings of 'Abdu'l-Bahá* 223)

In another instance, 'Abdu'l-Bahá expresses the eternal
nature of the Gospel's message:

No matter how much the world of humanity advances
in material civilization, it is nevertheless in need of
the spiritual development mentioned in the Gospel.
(*Promulgation* 205)

And the Guardian, in a forceful statement of Bahá'í beliefs
concerning Christianity, writes:

let it be stated without any hesitation or equivocation
that . . . the divine inspiration of the Gospels is fully
recognized. (*Promised Day* 109)

This passage is especially significant because it is as a clear
example of how the Guardian himself summed up the Bahá'í
position on the Gospel.· He says the Bahá'í affirmation is
stated without any 'hesitation'. This is underlined by the fact
that it is not qualified by statements accommodating theories

or controversies about the Gospel. Moreover, the position is stated without 'equivocation'. This is, in part, seen in the fact that there is no mention of, or emphasis on, any issues involving actual errors or alleged errors in early or current texts of the Gospel. The 'divine inspiration' is 'fully' - not partially - recognized. Furthermore, he does not state that this affirmation is a secondary or minor Bahá'í teaching, but is among:

> the central, the solid, the incontrovertible principles
> that constitute the bedrock of Bahá'í belief, which the
> Faith of Bahá'u'lláh is proud to acknowledge, which its
> teachers proclaim, which its apologists defend, which
> its literature disseminates, which its summer schools
> expound, and which the rank and file of its followers
> attests by both word and deed. (*Promised Day* 110)

These Bahá'í passages reflect an attitude towards the Bible which can be seen throughout the authoritative Bahá'í writings and talks of 'Abdu'l-Bahá. It is good to memorize examples of such verses, for they will rightly win the approval of many sincere Christians, effectively dispel Christian apprehensions, and seriously weaken any attempts by Christians to misrepresent the Bahá'í position.

Moreover, even though the Gospel does not contain all the words Jesus spoke to the Apostles or all the things that He did, this should not be used as an argument to cancel out the affirmations of the Gospel found in the sacred Bahá'í Writings or used as justification for asserting that the Gospel is in any way defective. The texts of the Gospel admit that it does not contain everything Christ did or said (e.g., John 21:25), but we also know that we do not possess all that Bahá'u'lláh revealed (*God Passes By* 121). Nevertheless, Bahá'u'lláh assures us that the 'testimony of Providence' has never been incomplete (*Certitude* 13-14). Whatever was essential to the salvation and guidance of people has been revealed.

In the next Chapter we will take a closer look at the issue of errors in the Bible and discuss what implications this issue has for our dialogues with Christians.

chapter
## 3

## THE AUTHENTICITY OF THE BIBLE

### THE EFFECTS ON THE BIBLE OF TRANSCRIPTION, TRANSLATION AND INTERPRETATION

There are a few passages in the Bahá'í writings on the Bible which some Christians may misunderstand as assaults on its integrity. In order to be prepared for such misunderstandings and to avoid misunderstanding Bahá'í beliefs about the Bible ourselves, we need to make a careful study of the writings concerning the authenticity of the Bible.

While affirming the Bible, the Bahá'í writings appear to back up some Christian scholars who claim that some minor errors have entered into some copies of the Bible during the process of transcribing and translating. 'Abdu'l-Bahá writes:

> as to thy question concerning the additions to the Old and New Testament: Know thou, verily, as people could not understand the words, nor could they apprehend the realities therein, therefore they have translated them according to their own understanding and interpreted the verses after their own ideas and the text fell into confusion. This is undoubtedly true. As to an intentional addition: this is something uncertain. But they have made great mistakes as to the understanding of the texts and the comprehending of the references and have therefore fallen into doubts, especially in regard to the symbolical verses. (*Tablets of Abdul-Baha Abbas* 609. This passage

is originally from a tablet translated by 'Alí-Kuli Khan.)

This passage is not entirely clear and could be interpreted as conflicting with the quotes mentioned earlier from 'Abdu'l-Bahá. It therefore needs to be carefully examined. 'Abdu'l-Bahá appears to be addressing three issues:

1. Errors entering the text during translation because of a lack of understanding of the original meaning of the words. This point He seems to be affirming.[29]

2. Additions to the Scriptures - which, according to this translation, He describes as 'uncertain'. This point is not clear, since He does not indicate whether or not He is referring to books some Christians consider uncanonical. Such books are not uncommon in the East. More probably, He may simply be referring to the uncertainty of current assertions about major intentional additions, assertions which are unproven.[30] Understood in this way, the statement can be perceived as a defence of the Bible against unproven theories.

3. Interpretation of the text. In this regard, He affirms that it has been misinterpreted.

---

29. It may be best to use caution in inferring too much from this translation. After several scholars possessing knowledge of Arabic stated that 'Ali Kuli Khan's translation of this passage was somewhat misleading, this writer asked the Bahá'í scholar Stephen Lambden to offer his opinion. He writes, 'It was the understanding of the text that fell into confusion not the text itself. The first part of 'Abdu'l-Bahá's answer to the question about *ziyádat* (increase in senses and meanings) deals solely with the growth (*ziyáda*) in fallible human understanding of the biblical text: not as the translation states, textual confusion'. He adds, 'It is my view that the translation is badly misleading, especially the first half of the paragraph in question' (from a letter to the author).

30. Certain minor additions and apparent alterations do appear in some early manuscripts (see, e.g., E.S. Buchanan, *The Records Unrolled*, 54-6). This is well known, so it is unlikely that 'Abdu'l-Bahá is referring to these when He says this is 'uncertain'. Because the manuscripts were geographically spread out and circulated, it is possible, as Bahá'u'lláh points out (*Certitude* 86), to

It should be emphasized that 'Abdu'l-Bahá has not said anything that at least some Christian scholars, including Evangelicals, have not also said.  Nor has He indicated that such errors have affected in any significant way the integrity of the Scriptures.  He states the 'text fell into confusion' because of misinterpretation.

It is true that there is confusion because of differing views among scholars concerning the translation of certain words.  This is easily seen, for there are numerous translations of the Bible and there are ongoing disputes over which is more accurate.  But again, with specific respect to translation, such confusion, while clearly existing, does not appear to have significantly altered the intended meaning. 'Fell into confusion' may mean that the words themselves became confused, no longer expressing the original and true meaning, but 'Abdu'l-Bahá's statement appears to attribute most of the confusion to misinterpretation, as seen in the statement 'they have made great mistakes as to the understanding of the texts and the comprehending of the references and have therefore fallen into doubts, especially in regard to the symbolical verses'.  About this there can be no doubt and 'Abdu'l-Bahá even describes the mistakes as 'great'.

These statements by 'Abdu'l-Bahá should be understood in the light of all His other statements about the Bible and other passages in the Bahá'í writings.  The overall message in the Bahá'í writings does not appear to support any

---

detect these instances, and this prevents such corruptions from entering into present texts. However, during 'Abdu'l-Bahá's life, a radical biblical criticism had emerged. The exponents of this school of thought, such as Timothy Colani and David Strauss, gained great notoriety and said much that shook people's beliefs in the authority of the Bible. An interesting evaluation of some of their writings can be found in Beasley-Murray's *Jesus and the Future*. Consequently, by 'uncertain' 'Abdu'l-Bahá may be suggesting the unproven nature of some of their more extreme claims, interpretations and assessments. Once again, this writer asked the Bahá'í scholar, Stephen Lambden to comment on this question. In a letter, he wrote 'A more accurate translation (it seems to me) at this point would be: "Now as to the [matter of] intentional additions (al-izdiyád ʿamadan [presumably to the text of the Bible]). This is a matter which is other than established" (ghair al-mathbút; "unproven" is also correct)'.

assertion that the texts of the Bible have undergone radical altering. Problems in the texts must therefore be minor.[31]

## THE INSIGNIFICANCE OF THE ISHMAEL/ISAAC DISCREPANCY

This is one specific issue which is pointed out in the Bahá'í writings as an error in the text of the Bible. Whether or not this error resulted from transcription or otherwise is not stated. This error concerns Genesis 22:9:

> Then they came to the place of which God had told him. And Abraham built an altar there and placed the wood in order; and he bound Isaac his son and laid him on the altar, upon the wood. (See also Heb. 11:17 and James 2:21)

Bahá'u'lláh, however, writes:

> The Voice of God commanded Him to offer up Ishmael as a sacrifice, so that His steadfastness in the Faith of God and His detachment from all else but Him may be demonstrated unto men. (*Gleanings* 76. See also *Epistle* 101.)

The following is the Guardian's own commentary on the discrepancy between the Genesis account and the account in Bahá'u'lláh's writings:

---

31. 'The worst of the many thousand MSS. [manuscripts] of the New Testament that have come down to us would be sufficient to establish every one of the miracles of the Lord: His birth - His suffering - His death - His resurrection - His ascension and the promise of His return. The variant readings, of which there are in the New Testament alone tens of thousands, none of them affect in any wise the import of the plain declarations on which the Christian Faith stands. The issues between the Western and non-Western texts are questions of the words chosen to express the facts - never of the facts themselves' (E.S. Buchanan, *The Records Unrolled* 53). Buchanan goes on to discuss some examples of the different types of variant readings found in early documents. Examples can also be found in Sir Frederic Kenyon's *Our Bible and the Ancient Manuscripts*, see Appendix 1 for 'Notable Various Readings' 332-42.

As to the question . . . in connection with
Bahá'u'lláh's statement in the Gleanings concerning
the sacrifice of Ishmael; although this statement does
not agree with that made in the Bible, Genesis 22:9,
the friends should unhesitatingly, and for reasons that
are only too obvious, give precedence to the sayings of
Bahá'u'lláh which, it should be pointed out, is fully
corroborated by the Qur'án which book is more
authentic than the Bible, including both the New and
the Old Testaments. The Bible is not wholly
authentic, and in this respect is not to be compared
with the Qur'án, and should be wholly subordinated
to the authentic writings of Bahá'u'lláh. (*Lights of
Guidance* 370)

In reflecting on this issue, it is helpful to consider whether or
not such a discrepancy actually represents a significant error.
The Universal House of Justice has written:

In one of His Tablets 'Abdu'l-Bahá refers to this
discrepancy, and explains that, from a spiritual point
of view, it is irrelevant which son was involved. The
essential part of the story is that Abraham was willing
to obey God's command to sacrifice His son. Thus,
although the account in the Torah is inaccurate in
detail, it is true in substance. (From a letter to an
individual believer dated 19 July 1981)

'Abdu'l-Bahá's point indicates that the text can lack
complete authenticity but still be essentially correct with
regard to its spiritual message.

The Guardian states that we should accept the version
found in the Bahá'í writings 'for reasons that are only too
obvious'. From a secular historical point of view, the first

inclination is to accept the oldest document, which in this case would be the Old Testament. However, from the point of view of the religious believer such an approach is dubious. The Old Testament has undergone innumerable transcriptions over the centuries and the chance of such a minor error being introduced is entirely plausible, whereas many of Bahá'u'lláh's original writings still exist, can easily be authenticated, represent the latest Revelation from God, and have not been subject to such long processes of transcription.

Now, with reference to the Bible, it is important to note that Bahá'u'lláh Himself discusses the accusation that the Bible has been altered and corrupted. Bahá'u'lláh states that the corruption of the text, the 'alteration by the disdainful', has occurred 'only to particular cases' (*Certitude* 84). He then proceeds to provide an example of such a case. However, the example He uses clearly indicates that Bahá'u'lláh does not mean that in a few cases the actual text, or words, have been altered. Instead, Bahá'u'lláh indicates that such particular cases refer to the misinterpretation of the Scriptures (ibid. 84-6). With regard to the Muslim accusations about the Bible that Bahá'u'lláh addresses, He says that the Muslims have misunderstood what Muhammad meant by the word 'corruption'. He then adds that most instances of 'corruption', that is, misinterpretation of the Bible, referred to in the Qur'án, do not pertain to the Christians, but to the Jewish peoples.[32]

Bahá'u'lláh's discussion and defence of the Bible is particularly significant because He is fully aware of such minor discrepancies as the one involving Ishmael and Isaac. Yet,

---

32. Bahá'u'lláh writes, 'Moreover, most of the [Qur'ánic] verses that indicate "corruption" [i.e., misinterpretation] of the texts [i.e., of the Bible] have been revealed with reference to the Jewish people, were ye to explore the isles of the Qur'ánic Revelation' (*Certitude* 89, clarifications added).

when He refers to the corruption of the text, He does not include any mention of actual alterations of words such as in the Ishmael/Isaac instance. This suggests that Bahá'u'lláh did not regard this type of alteration in the Bible as significant. Therefore, to make an issue of the Ishmael/Isaac discrepancy with Christians, especially as a way of discounting the Bible, would be to show an inappropriate lack of appreciation for the Bible.

In Bahá'u'lláh's defence of the Bible, His focus is not solely on the Jewish and Christian leaders who rejected Muhammad because of their misinterpretation of the Bible. He is primarily rejecting the approach of the Muslims and their failure to correctly explain the Bible to the Jews and Christians. Bahá'u'lláh shows the arrogance of the Muslims who regarded 'them [Christians and Jews] as infidels', but failed themselves to demonstrate the truth of Muhammad by showing how He had fulfilled the prophecies of the Bible.

Here again is a lesson for us. We should not look down on Christians who do not accept Bahá'u'lláh, thinking that our presentation is so persuasive that any reasonable person will accept it. If someone remains unconvinced, we should 'beseech God to guide them' (*Epistle* 15) then continue to seek an even clearer way to give 'a reason for the hope' that is in us (1 Pet. 3:15).

## THE MEANING OF 'NOT WHOLLY AUTHENTIC'

If the original writings of the Prophets and Apostles existed, if they could be dated and if we could prove their authorship, the documents of the Bible could be completely authenticated. Or, if no discrepancies or variant readings appeared in early manuscripts and Bahá'u'lláh had specifically stated that the actual text, not just the teachings, was completely authentic, then we could base this degree of authenticity on both existing facts and His testimony and authority. However, none of these conditions exists.

It should be noted that the Guardian's indication that the Qur'án is more authentic and the Bible not wholly authentic raises two points: (1) The process or means of authentication; the fact that the Bible's actual texts cannot be fully authenticated, and (2) the error in Genesis which demonstrates that the text is not wholly authentic. However, these points do not mean that the original text was in error, nor do they mean that the rest of the text is not virtually authentic. Although the Guardian points out that the Bible is not wholly authentic with regard to every verse, this fact does not subvert the Bahá'í Faith's recognition of the Bible as an *authentic* Book of God:

> the Qur'án, the Bible, and our own Scriptures . . . only these can be considered authentic Books. (*Lights of Guidance* 381; from a letter written on behalf of the Guardian to an individual believer, 13 March 1950)

The easiest, most accessible and effective way to test whether the Bible is the Word of God is simply to respond to its spiritual message, which requires no scholarship or worldly knowledge. However, minor difficulties in the text involve numerous considerations often requiring a great amount of scholarly research. Christians themselves struggle with difficulties that appear to exist between the Old and New Testaments.[33] The focus of this book is not the opening of a door to conflict. Rather, the aim is to call attention to these issues so that if such points arise, we will be better equipped

---

33. See Josh McDowell and Don Stewart, *Answers to Tough Questions* 86-8. Josh McDowell and Don Stewart try to give persuasive explanations to account for why the Gospel of Matthew (Matt. 27:9-10) attributes a prophesy to Jeremiah that is actually given by Zechariah (Zech. 11:12-13). *The Encyclopedia of Bible Difficulties*, by Gleason Archer, is another very readable reference book that gives answers to a variety of different types of difficulties. These answers are also from a conservative Christian point of view.

to respond and not fall into the trap of overstating the significance of such errors. As always, the general points to be stressed are that the Bahá'í Faith:

- accepts and defends the Bible,

- regards the Bible as the 'sacred' and 'holy' 'Word of God', and

- encourages us to study the Bible.

## EMPHASIS ON THE BIBLE'S SPIRITUAL CONTENT IN THE BAHÁ'Í WRITINGS

We should also avoid endorsing the opinions of scholars who reject portions of the Bible. Relying on such scholarship to discount even the erroneous views of Christians can be self-defeating since these scholars often change their opinions, and have even rejected many portions of the Bible that are affirmed in the Bahá'í writings.[34]

Moreover, it cannot be over-stressed that this approach should be rejected as a convenient method of dismissing Christian questions or arguments that are based on Scripture, to hide our personal difficulty in understanding. Bahá'u'lláh, 'Abdu'l-Bahá and the Guardian provide many explanations of Christian doctrines such as the deity of Christ, the Resurrection, the Atonement and Jesus' Second Advent without ever rejecting a single verse of the Bible. On the contrary, they frequently cite the Bible when explaining

---

34. Students of the Bahá'í writings will discover that some of the main literary, historical and theological assumptions used by scholars who assert that radical errors or changes have entered into biblical texts are proved invalid and unpersuasive in the light of Bahá'u'lláh's Revelation. For example, many scholars reject all supernatural possibilities and assert that if a Biblical book, such as the Book of Daniel, contains prophecies that appear to have been fulfilled around 200 BC, then that book is a pretence that must have been written after 200 BC. They therefore consider the Book unauthentic and reject the internal evidence of the Book that indicates that it was written much earlier. Bahá'u'lláh's fulfilment of the prophecies in the book of Daniel as well as the fulfilment of Bahá'u'lláh's own prophecies vindicate both the legitimacy of prophecy and the inspiration of the Book of Daniel.

many Christian issues. Surely, this example should be followed when we discuss the Faith with Christians and attempt to answer their questions.

Anyone acquainted with the actual spiritual contents of the Bible will readily perceive its merits. Our approach to the Bible should be one of reverence, appreciation and humility. If we fail to understand a passage, we should guard ourselves against judging it as an 'unauthentic' part of the text. The Guardian's statements that the Bible is not wholly authentic were never intended as justification for ignoring the importance the Bible is given in the Bahá'í Writings or dismissing what we have trouble understanding.

This is not to argue that we should adopt an 'evangelical Protestant' view of the Bible in order to win the approval of conservative Christians. Rather, we should not compromise our own beliefs by dismissing the Bible because of the way it has been misinterpreted or by trying to win the approval of the people who have failed to appreciate it. Yet these points should not be construed as a rejection of the validity of scholarly research into the history and texts of the Bible.

The purpose of this examination is to establish the importance of the Bible in its relationship to the Bahá'í Faith. It is necessary to emphasize the spiritual content of the Bible, especially in our discussions with Christians and non-believers. It is this spiritual content that raises people to the life of faith and brings them closer to God. It is a source of guidance given to humankind to open the door of recognition to the truth of Bahá'u'lláh.

If we immerse ourselves in the Bahá'í writings and what 'Abdu'l-Bahá refers to as 'the glorious melodies of the Gospel' (*Secret of Divine Civilization* 36), we will discover the substance of the spiritual truths enshrined in the symbolism of Scripture, and we will cease to be pre-occupied with minor problems of accuracy and authentication.

# RESPONDING
# TO CHRISTIAN OBJECTIONS

**RESPONSES TO THE CHRISTIAN ASSERTION THAT
THE BIBLE IS THE ONLY AND LAST BOOK OF GOD**
Assertions that the Bible is the only and last Book containing
the true Word of God, are often bolstered by references to the
following verses:

> You shall not add to the word which I command you,
> nor take anything from it, that you may keep the
> commandments of the Lord your God which I
> command you. (Deut. 4:2)

> if anyone preaches any other gospel to you than what
> you have received, let him be accursed. (Gal. 1:9)

> For I testify to everyone who hears the words of the
> prophecy of this book: If anyone adds to these things,
> God will add to him the plagues that are written in
> this book. (Rev. 22:18)

We will present four ways for responding to Christians
who believe the Bible is the only and last Book containing
the Word of God. Briefly, these approaches are as follows:

- explain and demonstrate that the Bahá'í writings are
  one with the Bible,

- examine the verses, such as Deuteronomy 4:2, Galatians 1:9, and Revelation 22:18 to explain their contexts and show that they do not teach the finality of the Bible,

- stress the moral contradiction apparent in the belief that a loving God would only reveal His Word for a select group of people, and

- point out prophecies suggesting that with Jesus' Second Advent there will be a new Revelation from God

## THE BAHÁ'Í WRITINGS AND THE BIBLE ARE ONE IN SPIRIT

To convey that Bahá'í Scripture is one with the Bible, it is best to first emphasize the Bahá'í acceptance of the Bible. Having stressed this, we should explain that even though the Bahá'í writings are not the same as the Bible, they differ in the same respect that the Old differs from the New Testament. The Bible, the Qur'án and the Bahá'í writings all have a 'correlative character' (*Promised Day* 107). They express the same spirit, come from the same Source with essentially the same purpose. Bahá'ís neither reject the Bible in order to assert the supremacy of the Bahá'í writings nor believe that the spirit of biblical Scripture is in any way contrary to the Bahá'í teachings. 'Abdu'l-Bahá states:

> The Cause of Bahá'u'lláh is the same as the Cause of Christ. It is the same Temple and the same foundation. (*Bahá'í World Faith* 400)

Bahá'u'lláh states that all the Prophets utter the 'same

speech', and proclaim 'the same Faith' (*Certitude* 153-4).
And the Guardian writes:

> the Faith of Bahá'u'lláh - if we would faithfully
> appraise it - can never, and in no aspect of its
> teachings, be at variance, much less conflict, with the
> purpose animating, or the authority invested in, the
> Faith of Jesus Christ. (*World Order* 185)

All of these statements express the view that there is an
essential oneness between the Bahá'í Faith and Christianity.

Paul states that, 'if anyone preaches any other gospel to
you than what you have received, let him be accursed'
(Gal. 1:9). The word 'gospel' means 'good news', a term
which is derived from the Book of Isaiah (61:1-2). Jesus
quotes this verse (see Luke 4:18-19) and in this way He
indicates that He has come to preach the Gospel, that is,
the 'good news'.

These passages (Isa. 61:1-2; Luke 4:18-19) also offer a
type of definition concerning the message of the Gospel. It is
a message of how, through the ministry of Christ, we attain
deliverance and liberty from the captivity of sin, a message
that is affirmed and preached in the writings of the Apostles.
This message is also affirmed in the Bahá'í writings in the
recognition of Christ, through whose sacrifice, Bahá'u'lláh
says, 'a fresh capacity was infused into all created things'.
Bahá'u'lláh adds:

> We testify that when He came into the world, He
> shed the splendor of His glory upon all created things.
> Through Him the leper recovered from the leprosy of
> perversity and ignorance. Through Him, the
> unchaste and wayward were healed. Through His
> power, born of Almighty God, the eyes of the blind

were opened, and the soul of the sinner sanctified.
(*Gleanings* 86)

Thus, the Bahá'í writings preach the same 'Gospel', or
good news, about Christ, and the same message of the
Apostles, but in the context of the recognition that the
promises of Jesus and His prophecies concerning His return
were fulfilled in the Person of Bahá'u'lláh. In this sense the
'good news' is new or, put another way, the Bahá'í writings are
a 'New Gospel'.

Moreover, from the Bahá'í point of view, the Bible and
the Bahá'í writings are all Scripture. As we have noted, Paul
says:

All Scripture is given by inspiration of God and is
profitable for doctrine, for reproof, for correction, for
instruction in righteousness. (2 Tim. 3:16)

How can we determine what is Scripture if not by its spiritual
influence, consistency with the spirit of former Scriptures,
and its claims? The fact that the Bahá'í writings are
profitable for teaching, for reproof, for correction and for
instruction in righteousness testifies to their inspiration.

## BIBLICAL TEACHINGS ON 'THE ONLY AND LAST BOOK OF GOD'

In order to address the argument that the Bible is the only and
last book of God, we need to examine the biblical verses that
form the basis of the argument. In the examples commonly
referred to (Deut. 4:2 and Rev. 22:18), the real intentions of
the verses are warnings against false teachings. These verses
also prohibit unauthorized additions to, and deletions from, the
inspired texts. Deuteronomy 4:2, pertaining to the law of
Moses, is a warning directed at the people - not at future

Prophets appointed by the authority of God. If it was also directed at future Prophets, it could be argued that all the Scriptures of the Prophets coming after the Book of Deuteronomy were also additions that should be rejected. If the warning in Deuteronomy 4:2 does not pertain to Isaiah, Ezekiel, or even the New Testament, why should it be applied to the Bahá'í writings? Consequently, this prohibition must logically concern unauthorized human additions to, and deletions from, the laws revealed by Moses.

Even though the Prophets who came after Moses did not add to or delete from the law, changes did occur in the New Testament. For example, according to the law, the penalty for adultery was death by stoning (Deut. 22:21-4) yet Christ annulled this punishment. Similarly, if anyone worked on the Sabbath day 'he shall surely be put to death' (Exod. 31:14-15). These are the explicit teachings of the Old Testament. However, as a result of Jesus' teachings (John 8:3-11) and because, according to Scripture, He rose from the dead on the first day of the week, the Sabbath was changed from Saturday to Sunday. Hence Christian practices differ from those specifically prescribed in the Old Testament.

Moses said, 'You shall not add to the word which I command, nor take anything from it' (Deut. 4:2) so how could Jesus annul the penalty for adultery? Jesus said:

> Do not think that I came to destroy the Law or the Prophets. I did not come to destroy but to fulfil. For assuredly, I say to you, till heaven and earth pass away one jot or one tittle will by no means pass from the law till all is fulfilled. (Matt. 5:17-18)

How are we to understand these words in the light of the changes we know Christ made? The answer is given by Paul when he said, 'the letter kills but the spirit gives life' (2 Cor. 3:6). The letter of the law changes, but the spirit does not. Christ kept the spirit of the law.

Our focus should be on the spirit and essence of the Bible's message. Although Christ changed the letter of the law, in doing so he upheld its essential spirit. In fact, the change was necessary for that spirit to be upheld. The meaning of Deuteronomy 4:2 was not violated by Christ. In the same way, the writings of Bahá'u'lláh uphold and reflect the same eternal spirit of the Gospel.

In every age the Manifestations of God teach what is required to promote the knowledge of God and fellowship among the people. These two goals embody the spirit and essence of the Law. All the teachings and laws revealed in each age provide whatever is necessary to fulfil these two goals. However, the safeguard of these primary objectives in each age sometimes requires changing, adding or abrogating some laws.

Another verse some Christians appeal to when asserting that no additional Scripture will exist is Revelation 22:18. However, in this passage, John specifically refers to 'the words of the prophecy of this book' indicating that no one should add or take away (see Rev. 22:19) from the prophecy of the Book of Revelation. The Bahá'í writings in no way take away or add prophecies, or anything, from either the Book of Revelation or any Book of the Bible. On the contrary, Bahá'ís see the Bahá'í Faith as fulfilling the prophecies of the Bible.

## WHY GOD WOULD NOT WITHHOLD GUIDANCE FROM THE REST OF THE WORLD

The belief that the Bible is the only Word of God contradicts the nature of God. It also contradicts the clear evidences of, and claims made in, other Scriptures and Holy

Books.  How could it be that God's all-loving nature and grace would embrace only a small group of humanity? Bahá'u'lláh writes:

> the manifold bounties of the Lord of all beings have, at all times, through the Manifestations of His divine Essence, encompassed the earth and all that dwell therein.  Not for a moment hath His grace been withheld, nor have the showers of His loving-kindness ceased to rain upon mankind. (*Certitude* 14, see also 90)

The narrow exclusivity of the Christian interpretation is, moreover, not consistent with the nature of God's love described in the Bible.  Peter taught:

> God shows no partiality.  But in every nation whoever fears Him and works righteousness is accepted by Him. (Acts 10:35)

This verse testifies to God's love and justice towards all people and conveys the same spirit found in Bahá'í teachings. If the followers of other religions fear God and 'work righteousness' as a consequence of their adherence to the Holy Books of their faiths, should the merit of their Scripture not be recognized and the generating Source of such guidance wondered at?

The Gospel teaches that Jesus is 'the true Light which gives light to every man who comes into the world' (John 1:9) and that 'the grace of God that brings salvation has appeared to all men' (Titus. 2:11).  These teachings also reflect God's love for all humankind.  Because Bahá'ís believe the 'true light' of Christ is the same light found in all the world's great religions, they believe this love truly does embrace all the world for all times. These biblical teachings show that it is not consistent with the nature of God to assert that the Bible is the only Book imparting the Word of God to humankind. As 'Abdu'l-Bahá states,

> If a Christian sets aside traditional forms and blind imitation of ceremonials and investigates the reality of the Gospels, he will discover that the foundation principles of the teachings of Christ were mercy, love, fellowship, benevolence, altruism, the resplendence or radiance of divine bestowals, acquisition of the breaths of the Holy Spirit and oneness with God. Furthermore, he will learn that Christ declared that the Father 'maketh his sun to rise on the evil and on the good, and sendeth rain on the just and on the unjust'. The meaning of this declaration is that the mercy of God encircles all mankind, that not a single individual is deprived of the mercy of God, and no soul is denied the replendent bestowals of God. (*Promulgation* 444)

Finally, the Bible itself suggests that it is not the last Word of God to be spoken on this earth. According to Scripture, the Bible teaches that when Christ returns He will 'make all things new' (Rev. 21:5), and that 'He will teach us His ways' (Isa. 2:3). These prophecies suggest that, even though the spiritual truth of the Bible will not change, Christ will, nevertheless, again teach 'His way' but in a 'new' or different expression.[35]

---

35. We may also wish to refer to John 14:26 and 16:12-13, but bear in mind that Christians interpret these verses as references to the Holy Spirit descending upon the Apostles at Pentecost (Acts 2:1-4). The Bahá'í teachings maintain that John 14:26 and 16:12-13 refer to the Second Advent, when Christ will guide us into all truth, a prophecy Bahá'ís believe has been fulfilled by Bahá'u'lláh (*Some Answered Questions* 124-5. See also *Tablets of Bahá'u'lláh* 11).

**BIBLICAL REFERENCES FOR PART ONE**
If we choose to make an outline in our Bibles of the biblical information in Part One, we can use a yellow marker and record the following information according to the method described in Volume One of this series, *Understanding Biblical Evidence.*

> Answer to the argument that there can be no changes or additions to Scripture (Deut. 4:2; Rev. 22:18):
>> Deut. 22:21-4: the penalty for adultery
>> John 8:3-11: Jesus changes penalty prescribed in the Old Testament
>> Matt. 5:17-18: Jesus changes letter of law only
>> 2 Cor. 3:6: the letter kills
>
> Verses that support the belief that God would not show partiality to only one select group of people, depriving all others of Scripture:
>> Acts 10:35
>> John 1:9
>> Titus 2:11
>
> Biblical verses that suggest there will be more Scripture to come after the New Testament:
>> Isa. 2:3
>> Rev. 21:5
>> John 14:26 and 16:12-13

Remember, these verses are not entirely self-explanatory with regard to the questions we have discussed. Study carefully the arguments offered in order to learn how these verses relate to the answers we are trying to communicate.

As we have seen, the authority of the Bible is of central importance to many Christians. In Part Two we will study the proposition put forward by some that the only reason the Bible, both Old and New Testaments, is really important is that it enables humankind to know the Person of Jesus Christ.

## part two

## THE DIVINITY OF CHRIST

### INTRODUCTION

In Chapter 5 we will briefly consider some aspects of the doctrine of the *deity* of Christ, also referred to as the *Incarnation*. In Chapter 6 we will respond to some common Christian arguments and examine the significance of the titles 'Son of God' and 'only begotten Son', and in Chapter 7 we will consider why a Manifestation of God can, in fact, claim to be God.

Understanding Christian beliefs about Jesus' nature is of special importance in the context of Bahá'í/Christian dialogues because such beliefs are frequently asserted to challenge views that are basic to the Bahá'í Faith. For example, since many Christians believe that Jesus is the Son of God, they commonly argue that He is superior to the Founders of all the other great religions of the world,[36] while the conservative Christians who believe that Jesus is an incarnation of God find it difficult to accept the Bahá'í belief that Christ, like Bahá'u'lláh, is essentially one of the Manifestations of God.[37]

---

36. A selection of Christian viewpoints concerning non-Christian religions can be found in *Christianity and Other Religions: Selected Readings* edited by John Hick and Brian Hubblethwaite. A conservative Christian argument for the superiority of Christ over the Founders of other religions can be found in *Jesus - A Savior or the Savior?* by Russell F. Aldwinckle.
37. The terms 'Manifestation of God' and 'Prophet' have been explained in Volume One of *Preparing for a Bahá'í/Christian Dialogue* 96-8.

# 5

## UNDERSTANDING
## THE RELATIONSHIP BETWEEN
## JESUS CHRIST AND GOD

### CHRISTIAN BELIEFS ABOUT JESUS

The doctrine of the Deity of Christ, stated simply, means that Christ is God. The other term, 'Incarnation', is derived from the Latin translation of the Bible, 'in carne' being a translation of the words 'became flesh' in John 1:14. This term expresses the belief that God became embodied in flesh (i.e., the body of Jesus). With regard to Christian doctrine, it is understood by some to mean that God became a 'God-man'[38] in the Person of Jesus by way of the virgin birth. How the one transcendent, unchanging and omnipresent God can assume the inherent limitations of a human form is not, and cannot be, adequately explained by this doctrine. Because such Christians believe Scripture supports this interpretation of the Incarnation, they have asserted that no contradiction exists. Rather, they have argued since early times that it is a *mystery* how God could be embodied in the flesh and still possess the exalted perfections we attribute to God.

In AD 451, a council of Christian theologians debated this issue and formalized their understanding of it into official dogma. Their conclusions are still accepted in the creeds of the Eastern Orthodox, Roman Catholic, and most Protestant

---

38. This is technically referred to as the 'hypostatic union'. Theologians have developed highly sophisticated terminology but in most cases it is unlikely that many Bahá'ís will ever need to know, or will ever encounter the use of, such terms.

Churches.[39]   However, a growing number of liberal theologians have recognized, and admitted, that it is not possible for God to truly assume a human form without necessarily ceasing to fully possess all divine attributes, such as omnipresence, which characterize the nature of God.  Rather than believe, like most Christians, that the Incarnation is an incomprehensible mystery, they reject it.  Unfortunately, some of these theologians also reject Jesus' divinity and assert that Jesus was only a man, although a very exceptional one.  The Bahá'í teachings, while agreeing that God is exalted above all corporeal limitations, cannot be identified with such an inadequate view of the greatness of Jesus Christ.

## POINTS OF AGREEMENT: BAHÁ'Í TEACHINGS ABOUT THE STATION OF CHRIST

Most Christians affirm that Christ was both human and divine, believing He possessed a perfect and sinless human nature and that He was God.  In some important respects Bahá'ís affirm both points.  Bahá'ís agree that, because Jesus was born of a woman, the Virgin Mary (*Certitude* 56), He possessed a human body and submitted to the conditions of that body (ibid 72) such as growth (Luke 2:40), hunger (Matt. 4:2), thirst (John 19:28), weariness (John 4:6) and sleep (Matt. 8:24), as well as human expressions of emotion, such as weeping (John 11:35).

Bahá'ís also accept Jesus' divine nature.  Expressing the Bahá'í position concerning Christianity, the Guardian writes 'the Sonship and Divinity of Jesus Christ are fearlessly asserted' (*Promised Day* 109).  Bahá'ís also recognize that inasmuch as Christ reflects the attributes of God, He can legitimately claim to be God (*Certitude* 178).  This second point we will discuss in more detail later in this section.

---

39. Shoghi Effendi mentions that mistaken concepts crept into Christianity during the first century and later became crystallized into accepted dogmas. (See *World Order* 138.)

The recognition of Jesus' Sonship and Divinity is apparent in many passages throughout the Bahá'í writings, but some Christians believe this recognition falls short for, according to Christian doctrine, Jesus is more than divine: He is God. In other words, there is a distinction that concerns the difference between possessing the attributes of God's divinity and actually being God in essence. Bahá'ís believe that through the physical and historical Person, Jesus Christ, the divine attributes of God were made manifest to the world, but that God's essence is too transcendent to be fully embodied in flesh. From the Bahá'í point of view, this is the meaning of the Word becoming flesh, - the incarnation - as described in the first chapter of the Gospel according to John.

# 6

## RESPONDING TO CHRISTIAN ARGUMENTS ABOUT JESUS

**RESPONSES TO THE ARGUMENT THAT THE APOSTLES TAUGHT THAT JESUS IS THE 'INCARNATION OF GOD'S ESSENCE'**

The Christian belief that Jesus is God in essence, in the flesh, is based primarily on interpretations of the New Testament and, particularly, on statements made by the Apostles John and Paul. The following verses are one source of this belief; verse 1:14 of John is where the term 'incarnation' originates:

> In the beginning was the Word, and the Word was with God, and the Word was God. (John 1:1)

> And the Word *became flesh* and dwelt among us, and we beheld His glory, the glory as of the only begotten of the Father, full of grace and truth. (John 1:14, emphasis added)

Briefly, the Christian understanding is as follows: the Word is equated with God (John 1:1) and, according to the text, 'became flesh' (John 1:14, Latin, *'in carne'*) in the Person of Christ. Christians believe this means God 'incarnated' both His essence and attributes, that is, made Himself come into the world in the flesh. In addition to these verses, Christians also point out that Paul has written:

Christ Jesus, who, being in the form of God, did not consider it robbery to be equal with God (Phil. 2:5-6; see also Col. 2:9).

From a Bahá'í point of view, this passage can be understood as referring to the divine perfections: the light of God, but not the complete Essence of God. Other biblical passages can be understood in the same way. For example, when it states God became flesh, the meaning is that the Word of God and perfections of God became manifest in the flesh, that is, in the Person of Jesus. Jesus lived perfectly the teachings He preached, and thus He is the Word.[40]

Paul writes that Christ is the 'image of the invisible God' (Col. 2:15). Paul does not say that He is the incarnation of the invisible essence of God. When Paul states that Jesus is 'in the form of God' we can assume 'form' to mean divine perfections, since God does not have a physical form. In this respect, to say 'equal with God' can be understood to mean what Bahá'u'lláh expresses with these words:

Whatsoever is applicable to them [the Manifestations of God] is in reality applicable to God, Himself, Who is both the Visible and the Invisible. (*Certitude* 142)

The attributes of God, such as His omnipresence, make it impossible for finite creatures, like ourselves, to comprehend His Being. Because of God's nature, God is beyond containment in the visible world. But because signs and evidences of God are evident in all things, we are able, within our own limited perception, to perceive God in the

---

40. John the Baptist first referred to Christ as the Word, a title affirmed by Bahá'u'lláh in the *The Book of Certitude* 64. 'Abdu'l-Bahá also refers to Christ as 'the Word of God' (*Promulgation* 154-5, 212).

visible world. Thus, God can be perceived in the world but not contained in the world. 'Abdu'l-Bahá provides this explanation:

> the Word and the Holy Spirit, which signify the perfections of God, are the divine appearance. This is the meaning of the verse in the Gospel which says: 'The Word was with God, and the Word was God'; for the divine perfections are not different from the Essence of Oneness. The perfections of Christ are called the Word, because all the beings are in the condition of letters, and one letter has not a complete meaning; whilst the perfections of Christ have the power of the Word, because a complete meaning can be inferred from a Word. As the Reality of Christ was the manifestation of the divine perfections, therefore it was like a word. Why? Because He is the sum of perfect meanings. This is why He is called the Word. (*Some Answered Questions* 241)

The Bahá'í argument rests on the simple logic that an infinite God is uncontainable, especially in a finite physical form such as a human body. However, the perfections of God, His attributes, can be and are reflected in the human form of the Prophets and Manifestations. In fact, the Bahá'í belief is that all humans must strive to reflect these perfections (*Certitude* 101; *Promulgation* 69).

According to the Bahá'í teachings, if the infinite God were reduced to a finite form, He would cease to be God. The Guardian writes:

> that invisible yet rational God Who, however much we extol the divinity of His Manifestations on earth,

can in no wise incarnate His infinite, His unknowable, His incorruptible and all-embracing Reality in the concrete and limited frame of a mortal being. Indeed, the God Who could so incarnate His own reality would, in the light of the teachings of Bahá'u'lláh, cease immediately to be God. (*World Order* 112)

Support for this transcendent view of God can be seen in Solomon's statement:

But will God indeed dwell on the earth? Behold, heaven and the heaven of heavens cannot contain You. (1 Kings 8:27)

Despite such biblical teachings, many Christians believe that they must accept the traditional understanding of the Incarnation (i.e., meaning the incarnation of God's essence) because they believe Jesus made statements implying this doctrine.

## RESPONSES TO THE ARGUMENT THAT JESUS CLAIMED TO BE THE 'INCARNATION OF GOD'S ESSENCE'

To support the Christian arguments that Jesus is God's essence incarnate, Christians point out that Jesus said that He was one with God. The following verses testify to this claim:

I and My Father are one. (John 10:30)

If I do not do the works of My Father, do not believe Me; but if I do, though you do not believe Me, believe the works, that you may know and believe that the Father is in Me, and I in Him. (John 10:37-8)

If you had known Me, you would have known My
Father also; and from now on you know Him and
have seen Him. (John 14:7)

Even though Jesus states He is one with God, from a Bahá'í
point of view this oneness does not mean that Jesus is the
incarnation of God's essence.

'Abdu'l-Bahá explains the meaning of these passages by
analogy. He likens God to the sun, the Holy Spirit or
perfections of God to the light of the sun, and Jesus Christ to
a perfect mirror. This analogy, 'Abdu'l-Bahá explains, is
applicable to all Manifestations of God:

These holy Manifestations or Prophets of God are as
mirrors which have acquired illumination from the
Sun of Truth, but the Sun does not descend from its
high zenith and does not effect entrance within the
mirror. In truth, this mirror has attained complete
polish and purity until the utmost capacity of
reflection has been developed in it; therefore, the Sun
of Reality with its fullest effulgence and splendour is
revealed therein . . . The Sun of Divinity and of
Reality has revealed itself in various mirrors. Though
these mirrors are many, yet the Sun is one. The
bestowals of God are one; the reality of the divine
religion is one. Consider how one and the same light
has reflected itself in the different mirrors or
manifestations of it . . . For instance, the Sun of
Reality revealed itself from the Mosaic mirror. The
people who were sincere accepted and believed in it.
When the same Sun shone from the Messianic mirror,
the Jews who were not lovers of the Sun and who
were fettered by their adoration of the mirror of Moses
did not perceive the lights and effulgences of the Sun

of Reality resplendent in Jesus; therefore, they were deprived of its bestowals. Yet the Sun of Reality, the Word of God, shone from the Messianic mirror through the wonderful channel of Jesus Christ more fully and more wonderfully. (*Promulgation* 114-15)

In another discourse 'Abdu'l-Bahá states:

This is what Jesus Christ meant when He declared, 'the father is in the son', the purpose being that the reality of that eternal Sun had become reflected in its glory in Christ Himself. It does not signify that the Sun of Reality had descended from its place in heaven or that its essential Being had effected an entrance into the mirror, for there is neither entrance nor exit for the reality of Divinity; there is no ingress or egress; it is sanctified above all things and ever occupies its own holy station. (*Promulgation* 173-4)

And again, 'Abdu'l-Bahá explains:

The Lord Christ said, 'He that hath seen Me hath seen the Father' - God manifested in man. The Sun (God) does not leave his place in the heavens and descend into the mirror, for the actions of ascent and descent, coming and going, do not belong to the Infinite, they are the methods of finite beings. In the Manifestation of God, the perfectly polished mirror, appear the qualities of the Divine in a form that man is capable of comprehending. (*Paris Talks* 26)

This analogy is also the means by which 'Abdu'l-Bahá explains the Three Persons of the Trinity (*Some Answered Questions* 129-31). 'Abdu'l-Bahá insists that this explanation is 'so logical that it can easily be grasped by all minds willing to give it their consideration' (*Paris Talks* 26). This analogy is expressed in the *Book of Certitude*, where Bahá'u'lláh refers to the Manifestations by such phrases as 'Mirrors reflecting the divine Essence' (ibid. 66), 'Mirrors reflecting the light of divine Unity' (ibid. 97), and 'the Mirrors that truly and faithfully reflect the light of God' (ibid.142). The concept of the Manifestations acting as mirrors reflecting the image of God rather than being God's essence in the flesh is also suggested by Paul's words when He refers to Christ as He 'who is the image of God' (2 Cor. 4:4). In another passage Paul says Christ is 'the image of the invisible God' (Col. 1:15) and that when we turn to Him, we are 'beholding *as in a mirror* the glory of the Lord' (2 Cor. 3:18, emphasis added).

## RESPONSES TO THE ARGUMENT THAT THE TITLE 'SON OF GOD' SUPPORTS THE BELIEF THAT JESUS IS THE 'INCARNATION OF GOD'S ESSENCE'

Some Christians believe that it is because of the Virgin Birth that Jesus is called the Son of God. They believe, as God's Son, Jesus inherited a divine nature.[41] Furthermore, they assert, the claim to be the 'Son of God' indicates an equality with God, as Jews also perceived it. (See, for example, John 5:17-18, 10:31-6.)

The Bahá'í writings affirm that Jesus was miraculously born of a virgin (*Certitude* 56; *Paris Talks* 47; *Lights of Guidance* 366). This view is also taught in the Qur'án. (3:47; 21:91; 66:12).[42] Moreover, the Bahá'í writings acknowledge that the title 'Son of God' is applicable to Jesus (*Some Answered Questions* 73; *Selections from the Writings of 'Abdu'l-Bahá* 40). According to the Bahá'í

---

41. See, for example, *Practical Christian Theology* 108-9.
42. See *Jesus in the Qur'án* 75-82.

teachings, however, the 'greatness of Christ is not due to the fact that He did not have a physical father, but to His perfections, bounties, and divine glory' (*Some Answered Questions* 103). Bahá'ís believe these perfections and divine glory are possessed by all the Manifestations of God (*Certitude* 103-4).

Some Christians believe that generation after generation inherit Adam's sin. On the basis of this doctrine of original sin, they argue that Jesus was sinless because He was born of a virgin, so escaping the inheritance of the sin of Adam through physical parents. Yet being born without sin did not prevent Adam from sinning. Consequently a Virgin Birth is no conclusive proof of sinlessness. Jesus' sinlessness cannot be attributed to the Virgin Birth either but, rather, is because He Himself chose never to sin during his life. The Bible testifies that Jesus was sinless (2 Cor. 5:21), and the Bahá'í teachings assert that all the Manifestations possess equally the perfections of God (*Certitude* 103-04) and are sinless (*Some Answered Questions* 195). 'Abdu'l-Bahá teaches that, if Jesus' greatness is due to having no earthly father, 'then Adam is greater than Christ, for he had neither father nor mother' (*ibid.* 103). In another passage 'Abdu'l-Bahá says:

> Be free from prejudice, so you will love the Sun of Truth from whatsoever point on the horizon it may arise! You will realize that if the Divine light of truth shone in Jesus Christ it also shone in Moses and in Buddha. The earnest seeker will arrive at this truth. This is what is meant by the 'Search after Truth'. . . 'Seek the truth, the truth shall make you free.' So shall we see the truth in all religions, for truth is in all and truth is one! (*Paris Talks* 137)

From the Bahá'í point of view the title 'Son of God' signifies a spiritual and not a physical relationship to God. All are created by God, but this does not mean that God has a physical reality. 'Abdu'l-Bahá points out the spiritual nature of the title 'Son of God' by demonstrating its applicability to the believers. He cites the following verses to support this view:

> But as many as received Him, to them He gave the right to become children of God, even to those who believe in His name: who were born, not of blood, nor of the will of man, but of God. (John 1:12-13)

'Abdu'l-Bahá explains:

> the expression which John uses in regard to the disciples, proves that they also are from the Heavenly Father. Hence it is evident that the Holy reality, meaning the real existence of every great man, comes from God, and owes its being to the breath of the Holy Spirit. (*Some Answered Questions* 103)

The passage 'Abdu'l-Bahá cites from John is very forceful, for it emphatically states that those who believe are not born of 'blood', 'flesh', or the 'will of man' but 'of God'. This teaching is also expressed by Paul, who writes:

> For as many as are led by the Spirit of God, these are sons of God. (Rom. 8:14)

And, again, John writes:

> Behold what manner of love the Father has bestowed on us, that we should be called children of God! (1 John 3:1. See also Rev. 21:7.)

The Bahá'í point of view can be supported by these Bible passages, indicating that the title 'Son of God' signifies a spiritual relationship to God. Although Jesus expresses this relationship in complete perfection, which distinguishes Him from His followers, the title is nevertheless applied to the believers as well. Moreover, it should be noted that a virgin birth is not a prerequisite for this title, inasmuch as Jesus' followers are spiritually born again but are still physically born of human parents.

**RESPONSES TO THE ARGUMENT THAT THE PHRASE 'ONLY BEGOTTEN SON' SUPPORTS THE BELIEF THAT JESUS IS THE 'INCARNATION OF GOD'S ESSENCE'**

Christians emphasize that Jesus is not only the Son of God, but the only 'begotten' Son of God and for this reason His Sonship is unique and fundamentally different from that of the believers, because He possesses the divine essence in common with God the Father. The terminology 'only begotten' is expressed in the following verse:

> For God so loved the world that He gave His only begotten Son, that whoever believes in Him should not perish but have everlasting life. (John 3:16)

Additional references can be found in John 1:14,18; 3:18; and 1 John 4:9. It should also be noted that Bahá'u'lláh uses the same terminology in connection with Christ:

> Christ exclaimeth: 'All dominion is Thine, O Thou the Begetter of the Spirit (Jesus).' (*Prayers and Meditations* 263)

One way of understanding the meaning of 'only begotten' is to view it in light of Jesus' station as a Manifestation of God.

'Only begotten' can expresses Jesus' unique relationship to God which, as with all Manifestations from God, distinguishes Him from the rest of humanity.

The uniqueness of Manifestations of God such as Christ, is evidenced by the way they reveal God to humankind. Bahá'u'lláh states that God 'can never be known except through His Manifestation' (*Gleanings* 49):

> The door of the knowledge of the Ancient Being hath ever been, and will continue forever to be, closed in the face of men. No man's understanding shall ever gain access unto His Holy court. As a token of His mercy, however, and as a proof of His loving-kindness, He hath manifested unto men the Day Stars of divine guidance [the Manifestations], the Symbols of His divine unity, and hath ordained the knowledge of these sanctified Beings to be identical with the knowledge of His own Self. Whoso recognizeth them hath recognized God. (*Gleanings* 49-50. See also *Certitude* 99-100.)

This passage suggests that the Manifestations are the only way humankind can gain access to the knowledge of God and develop the relationship with Him which it needs. Although Bahá'ís do not believe any one Manifestation has ever been the final and only way to God, they do believe they are the only channel. Bahá'u'lláh writes:

> since there can be no tie of direct intercourse to bind the one true God with His creation, and no resemblance whatever can exist between the transient and the Eternal, the contingent and the Absolute, He hath ordained that in every age and dispensation a pure and stainless soul be made manifest in the

kingdoms of earth and heaven. Unto this subtle, this mysterious and ethereal Being He hath assigned a twofold nature; the physical, pertaining to the world of matter, and the spiritual, which is *born of the substance of God Himself*. He hath, moreover, conferred upon Him a double station. The first station, which is related to His innermost reality, representeth Him as One Whose voice is the voice of God Himself . . . The second station is the human station, exemplified by the following verse 'I am but a man like you'. . . These Essences of Detachment, these resplendent Realities are the channels of God's all-pervasive grace. Led by the light of unfailing guidance, and invested with supreme sovereignty, they are commissioned to use the inspiration of Their words, the effusions of Their infallible grace and the sanctifying breeze of Their Revelation for the cleansing of every longing heart and receptive spirit from the dross and dust of earthly cares and limitations. Then and *only* then, will the Trust of God, latent in the reality of man, emerge, as resplendent as the rising Orb of Divine Revelation, from behind the veil of concealment, and implant the ensign of its revealed glory upon the summits of men's hearts. (*Gleanings* 66-7, emphasis added)

In this passage Bahá'u'lláh indicates that the 'only' way humankind can realize its true spiritual potential is through the Manifestations. He also indicates that these Manifestations are 'born of the substance of God Himself'. It can be said that They are the 'only' way 'born' of God by which humankind can truly be saved and know God. This is one way of understanding the meaning of 'only begotten Son', and of Jesus' words:

I am the way, the truth, and the life. No one comes to the Father except through Me. (John 14:6)

This message is also expressed by Bahá'u'lláh:

He that hath Me not is bereft of all things. Turn ye away from all that is on earth and seek none else but Me. I am the Sun of Wisdom and the Ocean of Knowledge. I cheer the faint and revive the dead. I am the guiding light that illumineth the way. (*Tablets of Bahá'u'lláh* 169)

Thus, we can see that Bahá'u'lláh's message expresses the same truths stated in the Bible. Jesus' distinction from the rest of humanity does not denote a distinction between the other Manifestations of God who also impart God's Word and reflect God's attributes. Because all the Manifestations of God mirror the same true Light of God, they are all one. Therefore, it is possible for each to claim to be the only way.[43]

---

43. This writer wishes to make no pretence with regard to being a scholar of Buddhist sacred texts. However, it appears that in Buddhist Scripture, the teachings of Buddha are also asserted as the 'one way'. See *Dhammapada*, ch. 10. Also in the *Maha Parinibbana Suttanta*, Buddha is recorded as stating that the 'Eightfold Path', which constitutes Buddha's most fundamental moral teachings, is the standard by which other doctrines and paths should be judged. See *Sacred Books of the Buddhist*, vol. 3, 'Dialogues of the Buddha' 166.

# 7

## THE PROPHETS
## AND THEIR CLAIM TO BE GOD

### WHY A PROPHET CAN CLAIM TO BE GOD

In light of the Bahá'í teachings we have examined in chapters five and six, is it correct to refer to Christ or any Manifestation as God? Did Jesus or any of the Manifestations actually claim to be God? Although Jesus never directly states that He is God, the Bible clearly asserts that the title is applicable to Him (Isa. 9:6). In fact, Jewish opposition to Jesus' claims (John 10:33) is difficult to understand in the light of Isaiah's prophetic attribution of the title 'Mighty God' to the awaited Messiah:

> For unto us a child is born, Unto us a Son is given. . .
> And His name will be called Wonderful, Counsellor,
> Mighty God. (Isa. 9:6)

Whether we believe this verse refers to the First or Second Advent of Christ makes no difference with regard to the point under consideration - the title 'Mighty God' is clearly applied to the expected Messiah, signifying a divine reality. Isaiah does not say that the Messiah will be Mighty God in the flesh, rather He shall be 'Mighty God'. in 'name'.

All the Manifestations of God indicate their exalted station but only when God commands them to do so. Consider these verses of Christ:

I do nothing of Myself; but as My Father taught Me, I speak these things. (John 8:28)

For I have not spoken on My own authority; but the Father who sent Me gave Me a command, what I should say and what I should speak. (John 12:49)

Any statement by Christ implying He was God would have been a response to God's command, as one speaking on God's behalf. Christ speaking as God is no different from Moses speaking as God when God commanded Him to say to the people:

And I have led you forty years in the wilderness. Your clothes have not worn out on you, and your sandals have not worn out on your feet; you have not eaten bread, nor have you drunk wine or similar drink; that you may know that I am the Lord your God. (Deut. 29:5-6)

There are also instances of the Báb speaking as God. Consider the following verse written by the Báb to the Manifestation of God Who was to come after Him - Bahá'u'lláh:

This is a letter *from God*, the Help in Peril, the Self-Subsisting, *unto God*, the Almighty, the Best Beloved. (*Selections from the Writings of the Báb* 6, emphasis added.)

Also, in the writings of Bahá'u'lláh there are statements where Bahá'u'lláh speaks as God:

Fear thou God. He Who heralded this Revelation hath declared: He shall proclaim under all conditions: 'Verily, verily I am God, no God is there but Me, the Help in Peril, the Self-Subsisting'. (*Tablets of Bahá'u'lláh* 43)

Dwelling on the glorification of Him Whom God shall make manifest - exalted be His Manifestation - the Báb in the beginning of the Bayán saith: He is the One Who shall proclaim under all conditions, 'Verily, verily I am God, no God is there but Me, the Lord of all created things. In truth all others except Me are My creatures. O My creatures! Me alone do ye worship.' (*Tablets of Bahá'u'lláh* 53)

During Our sojourn in 'Iráq, when We were at the house of one named Majíd, We set forth clearly for thee the mysteries of creation and the origin, the culmination and the cause there of. However since Our departure We have limited Ourself to this affirmation: 'Verily, no God is there but Me, the Ever-Forgiving, the Bountiful.' (*Tablets of Bahá'u'lláh* 143)

Bahá'u'lláh is not claiming to be the incarnation of God's essence, but rather the 'complete incarnation of the names and attributes of God' (*World Order* 112). Like Christ, He is speaking as One Who is the perfect reflection of all God's divine attributes. This distinction is apparent in the following verse:

When I contemplate, O my God, the relationship that bindeth me to thee, I am moved to proclaim to all created things 'Verily I am God!'; and when I consider my own self, lo, I find it coarser than clay! (*World Order* 113)

Furthermore, Bahá'u'lláh states:

> Were any of the all-embracing Manifestations of God
> to declare: 'I am God!' He verily speaketh the truth,
> and no doubt attacheth thereto. For it hath been
> repeatedly demonstrated that through their
> Revelation, their attributes and names, the
> Revelation of God, His name and His attributes, are
> made manifest in the world. (*Certitude* 178)

Since the Manifestations of God are like mirrors reflecting His
light and conveying His voice, it is not plausible for any of the
them to say, 'I am a god'. There is only one God speaking
through them all. When they speak - representing the one
God - they therefore state or imply 'I am God'.

## CONCLUSION TO PART TWO

The points we have studied in Part 2 show that the Scriptures
do not indicate that Jesus or any Manifestation of God is the
incarnation of God's essence but, rather, a Manifestation of
God's divine attributes and a Mediator of His Word. From
the Bahá'í point of view, misunderstandings regarding the
station of Christ have arisen from misinterpretations of the
words of the New Testament. These misunderstandings fail
to take the distinction between the divine attributes of God
and His transcendent Unknowable Essence fully into
account. The words of the Prophets as well as of the Apostles
do not impose on God the limitations of corporeal existence
but, rather, convey the message of Divine unity; that the
divine natures of Jesus and God are one, but the physical
nature of Jesus is not to be identified with God's essense
because God is exalted above the limitations inherent in
physical creation. With regard to the concept of Divine
unity, Bahá'u'lláh writes:

> The essence of belief in Divine unity consisteth in regarding Him Who is the Manifestation of God and Him Who is the Invisible, the Inaccessible, the Unknowable Essence as one and the same. (*Gleanings* 167)

It should be stressed that the Bahá'í point of view does not attempt to reject any portion of the Scriptures or to imply in any way that Christian misunderstandings about God's nature resulted because verses in the New Testament were in error. The Scriptures Christians cite to support their beliefs concerning the incarnation can be interpreted in the light of Bahá'u'lláh's revelation to mean the incarnation of the names and attributes of God.

It might seem that the difference between the Christian and Bahá'í understanding of the station of Christ simply involves a distinction between the terms 'manifestation' and 'incarnation', and between 'divinity' and 'deity', but this is not the case. To simply say that Bahá'ís reject the incarnation or deity of Christ is very misleading. Such distinctions of belief do not lie with terminology but with how the terminology is understood.[44] The terms 'incarnation' (from the Latin translation of the Gospel of John) and 'deity' (from the Greek, meaning *God*), and their relationship to Christ, are clearly based on the authority of verses in the Bible that are quoted and explained by 'Abdu'l-Bahá. We should always be careful not to allow a misunderstanding of Scripture, terminology and theology to give the mistaken impression that our Faith denies the inspired verses of the Bible.

Even saying that the difference is in the distinction between the 'attributes' and 'essence' of God has to be done

---

44. Shoghi Effendi says that 'to Israel He [Bahá'u'lláh] was neither more nor less than the incarnation of the Everlasting Father [Isa. 9:6]' (*God Passes By* 94).

with care, because the word 'essence' can be used in different contexts to mean the essence of the attributes, or 'the essence of the Word Itself' (*Selections from the Writings of 'Abdu'l-Bahá* 60). Bahá'u'lláh, for example, refers to Christ as the 'Essence of the Spirit' (*Certitude* 57; see also *Promised Day* 109).

When discussing this matter with Christians it is best to turn directly to the Bible. As we have seen, there are no central verses on this issue that inherently contradict Bahá'í teachings. Instead, many verses directly support the Bahá'í point of view. Moreover, the Bahá'í teachings do not require acceptance of ideas that appear to conflict with the nature of God as presented in the Bible. In most discussions with Christians we can therefore simply affirm the Scriptures and avoid much controversy that may stand in the way of discussing the proofs and teachings of Bahá'u'lláh. For example, if a Christian should ask, 'Do Bahá'ís believe that Jesus is the Son of God?' we can avoid much needless hairsplitting by simply quoting Bahá'u'lláh's words: 'Say this is the One Who hath glorified the Son and hath exalted His Cause' (*Tablets of Bahá'u'lláh* 12). The true spirit of the Bahá'í Faith is conveyed best by referring to the sacred writings of Bahá'u'lláh which contain many statements affirming and glorifying Christ.

In all cases it is best to entirely avoid becoming involved in discussions about the more abstruse and controversial aspects of Christian doctrines. The subtle differences of belief over issues such as the Incarnation have become far too complex to be easily resolved. In fact, when we encounter topics that can be controversial, it is usually unwise to pursue them at length hoping to discuss them until the other person accepts our point of view. Instead, our objective should be simply to show, when possible, that the Bahá'í view can be supported from the Bible. In the case of the Incarnation, we can also show that this doctrine is not the necessary or intended meaning of the Scriptures.

It is also important in our thinking and in our dialogues with Christians to keep in mind the extraordinary implications of the claim that Jesus is a 'Manifestation of God'. If God is the eternal Lord and Jesus is a Manifestation of God, then Jesus is a Manifestation of the eternal Lord. It is difficult to imagine how anyone could deny Jesus' eternal Lordship without denying that Jesus is a Manifestation of God. 'Abdu'l-Bahá said, 'His [Jesus Christ's] reality is everlasting and eternal; it hath neither beginning nor end' (*Promulgation* 282, 395). It is this reality of Jesus that indicates that He *is* a Manifestation of God.

### BIBLICAL REFERENCES FOR PART TWO
The following list of information is partially taken from this section. However some of the verses are added as supplementary evidence for our own study of this issue. This additional information can be used in our outline for future reference.

The significance of the Virgin Birth:
  'Abdu'l-Bahá's argument concerning Adam (*Some Answered Questions* 103)
The title 'Son of God' has a spiritual significance:
  John 1:12-13 believers born of God
  Rom. 8:14 'these are sons of God'
  1 John 3:1 and Rev. 21:7 'called children of God'
Jesus' relationship with God:
  1 John 4:12 'No one has seen God at any time'
  John 5:19 'The Son can do nothing of Himself'
  John 7:29 'He sent Me'
  John 8:28 'My Father taught Me'
  John 12:49-50 'as the Father told Me'

John 14:28 'My Father is greater than I'

Mark 13:32 'of that day and hour no one knows, . . .
   nor the Son'

1 Tim. 2:5 'one God and one Mediator'

2 Cor. 4:4 'Christ who is the image of God'

Col. 1:15 'He is the image of the invisible God'

Moses speaks as God:

   Deut. 29:1-6

God cannot be contained:

   1 Kings 8:27

God does not change:

   Mal. 3:6

*part three*

# THE
# SUBSTITUTIONARY ATONEMENT

**INTRODUCTION**
Christian beliefs about atonement pertain to why Christ gave His life on the cross and what effect this sacrifice has for those who believe. Because many Christians believe that Christ's sacrifice was necessary for our salvation and that only Christ could atone for us, they often fail to understand the reason for, and importance of, Bahá'u'lláh's sacrifice. For this reason it is important to understand the Christian concept and to be able to explain the significance of Bahá'u'lláh's sacrifice. In Chapter 8 we will learn about Christian concepts of atonement, salvation and grace, and consider some of the Bahá'í writings that address these issues. In Chapter 9 we will examine how the concepts of salvation and heaven relate to the sacrifices made by the Manifestations of God. Since many Christians object to some of the Bahá'í points of view on the subject of atonement, in Chapter 10 we will study how to respond to some of the more common objections.

# 8

## THE MEANING OF ATONEMENT

### CHRISTIAN BELIEFS CONCERNING ATONEMENT

The word 'atonement' is one of the few theological words that have an Anglo-Saxon origin. It means 'at-one-ment', to be at one with God, and is used to indicate the establishment of harmony between man and God. Because of human sin, humankind is not at one with God. Christians believe that Jesus' death on the cross was a sacrificial offering that atoned for humankind's sin. That is, God accepted Jesus' sacrifice on behalf of those who believe in Jesus.

Beliefs about atonement vary among Christians. Almost all Christians accept that Jesus died for the salvation of humankind, but how Jesus' death brings about salvation has never been fully agreed upon. However, we will not explore the historical roots or the various Christian theories about atonement, focusing instead on those parts of the Bible most frequently referred to by conservative Christians to express their beliefs about atonement.

Most conservative Christians emphasize that the Bible teaches that all people are sinners (1 Kings 8:46; Eccles. 7:20; Rom. 3:23). Sin is the violation of God's law, of which Adam's disobedience recorded in Genesis (Gen. ch. 3) is the primal expression. The Bible also teaches that 'the wages of sin is death' (Rom. 6:23). These verses are interpreted as meaning that all people are sinners and all have committed a violation for which they must be punished by 'death'.

The Christian point of view maintains that God's justice demands that the penalty be enforced but His mercy desires that humankind be forgiven. Consequently, God sent His Son as a ransom for humankind's sins. Instead of permitting everyone to suffer the penalty of death for his or her own sins, Jesus bore the penalty Himself for all humanity. Thus, Jesus offered Himself as a sacrifice to pay the penalty rightfully owed by humankind. God will accept this offering only on behalf of those who repent, and who believe that Jesus is the Christ and accept Him as their Saviour. Salvation, therefore, does not come through good works, but through grace. That is, it is given freely by God to those who accept and have faith in Jesus Christ.

Jesus' death on the cross was a substitute for the death that all humankind deserved to die and so is referred to as the 'substitutionary atonement'. This atonement is seen as a reconciliation between the offender (man) and the offended (God's law). Moreover, Christians believe that only Jesus, because of His sinlessness and because He was God's Son, qualified as an acceptable sacrifice and so could act on behalf of humankind.

## POINTS OF AGREEMENT: A BAHÁ'Í VIEW

The Bahá'í Faith, generally speaking, does not have formal doctrines in the same sense that Christians have and it is not possible, therefore, to cite a Bahá'í doctrine of atonement. However, we can examine the Bahá'í writings and observe passages that bear on this issue.

According to 'Abdu'l-Bahá it 'is true that He [Jesus] sacrificed Himself for our sake' (*Promulgation* 450). Bahá'u'lláh states that Jesus was sacrificed 'as a ransom for the sins and iniquities of all the people of the earth' (*Gleanings* 76) and that by sacrificing Himself 'a fresh capacity was infused into all created things' (ibid. 85). These are the most important points of agreement we can emphasize with Christians. By stressing these truths we can establish a firm foundation for discussing other related issues.

The Bahá'í teachings also agree that humankind cannot save itself by good deeds alone because if man rejects the Manifestation 'his work shall God bring to naught ... Man's actions are acceptable after his having recognized [the Manifestation]' (*Epistle* 61). The Báb also stated that 'deeds are secondary to faith' (*Selections from the Writings of the Báb* 133). The Bahá'í view also agrees that salvation is through the grace of God (*Gleanings* 76).

## DIFFERENCES BETWEEN THE BAHÁ'Í AND CHRISTIAN VIEW OF ATONEMENT

The Bahá'í point of view differs from some Christian beliefs about atonement in several important respects. Most notably, Bahá'ís believe that all the Manifestations of God sacrifice themselves for the redemption of humankind and are the channels of God's saving grace (*Certitude* 34). All God's Messengers accept persecution in order to spread God's Word, awaken humankind spiritually, and bring people to God. In so doing they offer themselves as a ransom, allowing humankind to become free from 'the bondage of self' (*Tablets of Bahá'u'lláh* 12) and attain to 'life everlasting' (*Certitude* 34).

The Manifestations of God are perfect and, having committed no crime, they therefore innocently suffer in order to bring us back to God. In this way they suffer (1) because of us and (2) for us. That is:

- Humankind, because of its perversity and sinfulness, persecutes and often kills the Manifestations of God (*Gleanings* 76). Hence, humankind deserves to be punished but, since it is the Manifestations who are persecuted, it can be said that they suffer what we deserve to suffer.

• The Manifestations accept this suffering out of love for us (*Promulgation* 257) and to demonstrate to us the path that can lead us nearer to God. (*Promulgation* 28, 372, 383)

Humankind has not earned this bounty, it is given freely, and we obtain it solely by the grace of God. As we will see, the role of God's grace and its relationship to salvation figures more prominently in Bahá'í writings than it does in some conservative Christian beliefs.

Besides the greater breadth in viewing the way God's grace has been brought into the world, other differences distinguish the Bahá'í view from some conservative Christian beliefs. These differences concern the understanding of:

• the role of deeds in humankind's salvation,

• the nature of sin, and

• the nature of salvation.

Of all the differences between Christian and Bahá'í views, God's grace is the most central. This fact has eluded some Christian writers who have criticized the Bahá'í Faith.

The Bahá'í emphasis on spiritual values and moral conduct has led some to portray the Bahá'í Faith as mistakenly convincing its adherents that they can buy their salvation, or their way into heaven, with good deeds. Some Christians regard this emphasis as a futile 'legalism': the 'buying' of one's salvation by good works, or gaining freedom from sin by becoming perfect through good deeds. It is as if someone having performed their quota of good deeds, could then turn to God and say 'Now You owe me heaven in return'.

Since human beings cannot attain absolute perfection they cannot completely free themselves from sin, and so, say these Christians, non-Christians will inevitably face the penalty of sin. Also, to those who accept the doctrine of original sin, non-Christians are condemned for the sin of an ancestor (Adam), of whom most non-Christians are unaware.[45] Some believe non-Christians have no escape from their sins, except through acceptance of Christ. This raises the question of the millions of people living and dying in lands the message of Christ never reached. Increasingly, many Christians have found this difficult to reconcile with their belief that God is just and truly loving. Consequently, various attempts have been made to solve and explain the difficulty.[46]

However, many conservative Christians argue that a broader concept of God's grace, such as that held by Bahá'ís, is not possible, insisting that it would conflict with God's justice, which requires sinners to be punished. On the other hand, to assume that the majority of humankind has been without a means to attain salvation presents an injustice that also conflicts with God's nature,[47] since it is obviously unjust to hold people accountable for not accepting Christ when they were not given any opportunity for, or choice of, rejection or acceptance. The Bahá'í writings offer a positive alternative to this outlook - the belief that God's grace is all encompassing - as expressed in the teaching of *Progressive Revelation*.[48]

45. The doctrine of Original Sin asserts that sin is passed on from generation to generation from the time of Adam.
46. Geoffery Parrinder, *Avatar and Incarnation, A Comparison of Indian and Christian Beliefs* 266-9.
47. Bahá'u'lláh states that God would not punish people for their disbelief if they had not received adequate testimony from any of the Manifestations. See *The Book of Certitude* 12-14.
48. A discussion of Progressive Revelation can be found in Volume One of *Preparing for a Bahá'í/Christian Dialogue*. Bahá'u'lláh says that it is through the Manifestations of God that 'the manifold bounties of the Lord of all beings have at all times . . . encompassed the earth and all that dwell therein' (*Certitude* 13).

In order to discuss these issues with Christians it is helpful to be aware of some of the many passages in the Bahá'í writings about God's grace.

## BAHÁ'Í WRITINGS CONCERNING GRACE, FAITH AND FORGIVENESS

According to the teachings of Bahá'u'lláh, God is the Source of all grace (*Gleanings* 8), God's grace is infinite (*Certitude* 95), and God's grace can 'never cease from flowing' (*Gleanings* 74). Bahá'u'lláh writes that the Manifestations of God are 'made manifest unto all men' as a result of God's grace (*Certitude* 9, also 34) and these Manifestations are 'the channels of God's all-pervasive grace' (*Gleanings* 67). This grace is the means by which all humankind can attain salvation:

> It is through the abundant grace of these Symbols of Detachment [Manifestations] that the Spirit of life everlasting is breathed into the bodies of the dead. (*Certitude* 34)

Bahá'u'lláh points out that because of humankind's sins, it deserves to die, but because of God's grace, it is protected from this fate:

> No man can ever claim to have comprehended the nature of the hidden and manifold grace of God; none can fathom His all-embracing mercy. Such hath been the perversity of men and their transgressions, so grievous have been the trials that have afflicted the Prophets of God and their chosen ones, that all mankind deserveth to be tormented and to perish. God's hidden and most loving providence, however, hath, through both visible and invisible agencies,

protected and will continue to protect it from the penalty of its wickedness. Ponder this in thine heart, that the truth may be revealed unto thee, and be thou steadfast in His path. (*Gleanings* 76)

And, in another passage, Bahá'u'lláh reiterates this truth with these words:

There can be no doubt whatever that if for one moment the tide of His mercy and grace were to be withheld from the world, it would completely perish. (*Gleanings* 68)

Bahá'u'lláh expresses His own role as a channel of God's grace to humankind in these words:

Let him who will, acknowledge the truth of my words; and as to him that willeth not, let him turn aside. My sole duty is to remind you of your failure in duty towards the Cause of God, if perchance ye may be of them that heed My warning. Wherefore, hearken ye unto My speech, and return ye to God and repent, that He, through His grace, may have mercy upon you, may wash away your sins, and forgive your trespasses. The greatness of His mercy surpasseth the fury of His wrath, and His grace encompasseth all who have been called into being and been clothed with the robe of life, be they of the past or of the future. (*Gleanings* 130)

In another passage, Bahá'u'lláh stresses the importance of belief and its effect upon the believer:

Whosoever acknowledged His truth and turned unto Him, His good works outweighed his misdeeds, and all

his sins were remitted and forgiven . . . Thus God
turneth iniquity into righteousness, were ye to explore
the realms of divine knowledge, and fathom the
mysteries of His wisdom. (*Certitude* 113-14)

From these passages, it is evident that if we acknowledge His
truth and turn to Him, all our sins are 'remitted and forgiven'
and that if we repent, God will 'through His grace' wash away
our sins and forgive our trespasses. Although Bahá'u'lláh states
that repentance and acknowledgement of His truth (i.e having
faith in Him) frees man from the penalty of past sins, does it
free him from future sins, and does this forgiveness also bring
eternal life? Bahá'u'lláh writes:

In like manner, whosoever partook of the cup of love,
obtained his portion of the ocean of eternal grace and
of the showers of everlasting mercy and entered into
the life of faith - the heavenly and everlasting life.
But he that turned away from that cup was
condemned to eternal death. By the terms, 'life' and
'death', spoken of in the Scriptures, is intended the
life of faith and death of unbelief. (*Certitude* 114)

In this passage Bahá'u'lláh shows the essential relationship of
faith to the attainment of 'everlasting life'. That any future
sins may also be forgiven is implied in the term '*everlasting
life*'. Also, in the many prayers Bahá'u'lláh revealed for the
believers, Bahá'u'lláh assures the faithful that God is 'Ever-
Forgiving' (*Prayers and Meditations* 5, 6, 17, 18, 22, 25, 26,
and so on). In one such prayer Bahá'u'lláh writes:

Glorified art Thou, O Lord, Thou forgivest at all
times the sins of such among Thy servants as implore
Thy pardon. (*Bahá'í Prayers* 82)

Bahá'u'lláh states that the ocean of God's forgiveness 'is boundless' (*Prayers and Meditations* 82). This can be seen in 'Abdu'l-Bahá's statement:

> It is even possible that the condition of those who have died in sin and unbelief may become changed - that is to say, they may become the object of pardon through the bounty of God, not through His justice - for bounty is giving without desert, and justice is giving what is deserved. (*Some Answered Questions* 269)

These passages demonstrate that humankind's salvation is obtained through the gift of God's grace. Furthermore, humanity receives this grace individually through repentance and belief. To repent means, literally, to think differently about things, to recognize one's error, and implies a real change in behaviour.[49]

However, if we receive the teachings of the Manifestation we are receiving God's grace, for they are a bestowal of God's grace given for humankind's happiness and betterment (*Synopsis and Codification* 12). We are saved by the grace of God, but this grace is received both by the act of faith and by the practising of God's commandments.

## FAITH AND DEEDS AND THEIR RELATIONSHIP TO SALVATION

Bahá'u'lláh states that faith is the first priority, followed by deeds, but this does not preclude the essential importance of deeds to a religious life:

> The first duty prescribed by God for His servants is the recognition of Him Who is the Dayspring of His

---

49. This is understood as inherent in the meaning of 'repent' as it is used in the New Testament. See *Vines Expository Dictionary of Biblical Words* 525.

Revelation and the Fountain of His Laws, Who
representeth the Godhead in both the Kingdom of
His Cause and the world of creation. Whoso
achieveth this duty hath attained unto all good: and
whoso is deprived thereof, hath gone astray, though
he be the author of every righteous deed. It
behooveth everyone who reacheth this most
sublime station, this summit of transcendent glory,
to observe every ordinance of Him Who is the
Desire of the World. These twin duties are
inseparable. Neither is acceptable without the
other. (*Synopsis and Codification* 11. See also *Tablets
of Bahá'u'lláh* 268.)

In this passage Bahá'u'lláh sets forth two duties, (1) the
acknowledgment of His truth and (2) the following of every
ordinance He has revealed. These duties, He states, are
inseparable and mutually conditional. However, if
Bahá'u'lláh has stated that salvation is secured by our faith
and the acceptance of our faith is conditional upon our
observance of every ordinance, then does the violation of
any ordinance cut us off from salvation and eternal life? In
the opinion of this writer, the answer is no. This conclusion
is based on this writer's understanding of Bahá'u'lláh's
overall message of salvation.

It is true that our deeds affect the state and quality of
our being, but the life of our faith is not necessarily
extinguished by a single misdeed. The human state of being
is never the station of absolute perfection (*Lights of
Guidance* 175; *Some Answered Questions* 267). The human
condition is, therefore, one of striving. We can repent for
failures and be forgiven, but we must not give up working
towards righteousness in order to remain faithful to God.
This aspect of striving is reflected in Paul's words:

Eternal life to those who by patient continuance in doing good seek for glory, honour and immortality. (Rom. 2:7)

Paul also teaches that good deeds are inseparable from faith. He writes that the grace of God that comes through faith does not remove the need for obeying the law:

What shall we say then? Shall we continue in sin that grace may abound? Certainly not! (Rom. 6:1)

He reiterates this point with these words:

What then? Shall we sin because we are not under law but under grace? Certainly not! (Rom. 6:15)

John also expresses the same importance of conduct:

Whoever abides in Him does not sin. Whoever sins has neither seen Him nor known Him. (1 John 3:6)

Even though the Bahá'í writings state that deeds are secondary to faith (*Selections from the Writings of the Báb* 133), secondary does not mean dispensable. As Paul says:

Do we then make void the law through faith? Certainly not, On the contrary, we establish the law. (Rom. 3:31)

Reflection on the meaning of salvation can help us better understand the role of deeds. This is the topic of the next chapter.

chapter
9

## THE MEANING OF SALVATION

**UNDERSTANDING THE TERMS 'HEAVEN' AND 'HELL'**
Generally speaking, salvation means to be saved from punishment or death, and hence to be assured of eternal life. In western religious terminology these alternative fates, and/or conditions, are often called 'Hell' and 'Heaven'. These terms are commonly used to refer to the fate of the individual soul after physical death. However, Bahá'u'lláh uses the two terms 'heaven' and 'hell' to express the condition of being spiritually near to or far from God:

> They say: 'Where is Paradise, and where is Hell?' Say: 'The one is reunion with Me, the other thine own self'. (*Epistle* 132)

This verse suggests a concept of Heaven (Paradise) and Hell independent of and transcending both time and place. Whether we think of heaven as a condition to be experienced by our present relationship to Bahá'u'lláh or as a state we will attain only after our physical death, it is impossible to imagine how heaven could ever be compatible with a sinful and unrighteous state of being. Even as sin brings sorrow into our lives now, it is apparent that sin would always be counter to any state of being or condition that might be understood as heaven.

The salvation brought about by the Manifestations of God is more than a grace assuring everlasting *existence*. It is also a grace which, through obedience to their teachings, makes eternal existence itself heavenly and spiritual. Bahá'u'lláh writes:

> These Essences of Detachment [the Manifestations], these resplendent Realities are the channels of God's all-pervasive grace. Led by the light of unfailing guidance, and invested with supreme sovereignty, they are commissioned to use the inspiration of Their words, the effusions of Their infallible grace and the sanctifying breeze of Their Revelation for the cleansing of every longing heart and receptive spirit from the dross and dust of earthly cares and limitations. Then, and only then, will the Trust of God, latent in the reality of man, emerge, as resplendent as the rising Orb of Divine Revelation, from behind the veil of concealment, and implant the ensign of its revealed glory upon the summits of men's hearts. (*Gleanings* 67)

In this passage Bahá'u'lláh sets forth how the 'cleansing' of the heart is related to the spiritualization of humankind. In other words, the Prophets are not only channels for remitting the penalty of our past and present shortcomings and sins, they are also channels through which God guides humankind towards a heavenly life without sin. The teachings of the Prophets are essential to these spiritual processes. 'Abdu'l-Bahá writes that, because of human attachment to the world, people deprive themselves of spiritual bounties. He states:

> attachment to the world has become the cause of the bondage of spirits, and this bondage is identical with sin. (*Some Answered Questions* 142)

This attachment is due to humankind's physical nature and, in this sense, sin 'has been transmitted from Adam to his posterity' (ibid.). 'Abdu'l-Bahá explains:

> It is because of this attachment that men have been deprived of the essential spirituality and exalted position. When the sanctified breezes of Christ, and the holy light of the Greatest Luminary [Bahá'u'lláh] were spread abroad, the human realities, that is to say, those who turned towards the Word of God and received the profusion of His bounties, were saved from this attachment and sin, obtained everlasting life, were delivered from the chains of bondage, and attained to the world of liberty. They were freed from the vices of the human world, and were blessed by the virtues of the Kingdom. This is the meaning of the words of Christ, 'I gave my blood for the life of the world' [John 6:51-4]; that is to say: I have chosen all these troubles, these sufferings, calamities, and even the greatest martyrdom, to attain this object, the remission of sins: that is, the detachment of spirits from the human world, and their attraction to the divine world; in order that souls may arise who will be the very essence of the guidance of mankind, and the manifestations of the perfections of the Supreme Kingdom. (ibid.)

'Abdu'l-Bahá has equated sin with attachment to things that impel man away from spiritual life. Paul suggests the same truth with these words:

> But I see another law in my members warring against the law of my mind, and bringing me into captivity to the law of sin which is in my members. (Rom. 7:23)

The following verses also express this same truth:

> For those who live according to the flesh set their minds on the things of the flesh, but those who live according to the Spirit, the things of the Spirit. For to be carnally minded is death, but to be spiritually minded is life and peace. (Rom. 8:5-6)

> For if you live according to the flesh you will die, but if by the Spirit you put to death the deeds of the body, you will live. (Rom. 8:13)

Paul equates being spiritually-minded with life and peace, while carnal living is equated with death. With these words, Paul gives a spiritual significance to the terms 'life' and 'death'. He seems to be indicating that death is not the passing away of the body and life is not merely physical existence. He associates the orientation of the individual towards carnal or spiritual practice with these states of existence. 'Abdu'l-Bahá explains:

> A certain disciple came to Christ and asked permission to go and bury his father. He answered, 'Let the dead bury their dead' [Matt. 8:22]. Therefore, Christ designated as dead some who were still living - that is, let the living dead, the spiritually dead, bury your father. They were dead because they were not believers in Christ. Although physically alive, they were dead spiritually. This is the meaning of Christ's words, 'that which is born of the flesh is flesh, and that which is born of Spirit is spirit' [John 3:6]. He meant those who were simply born of the human body were dead spiritually, while those quickened by the breaths of the Holy Spirit were living and eternally

alive. These are the interpretations of Christ Himself. (*Promulgation* 245-6)

With 'Abdu'l-Bahá's explanation in mind, let us consider the spiritual significance of Paul's words:

> For the wages of sin is death, but the gift of God is eternal life in Christ Jesus our Lord. (Rom. 6:23)

The foregoing words from Paul, and the explanation by 'Abdu'l-Bahá, suggest that the meaning of 'death' spoken of in Scripture is not physical death followed by eternal anguish for disbelievers. Nor is 'eternal life' limited to a state after physical death.

In Scripture both terms, 'life' and 'death', have symbolic meanings concerned with the condition of the soul. We can be physically alive in this world yet spiritually dead. Heaven and hell are terms that can be applied both to life here and the condition of a soul after physical death. Righteousness and good conduct are important to salvation because salvation begins with our spiritual well-being in this life. This view suggests that eternal life, heaven and salvation are all interrelated - different terms characterizing the state of the believer's spiritual existence.

It is helpful to note that the fate of the believers, according to the Bible, is eternal life (John 3:15), and the fate of disbelievers is eternal hell (Matt. 18:8; Rev. 20:10), but in both cases the fate is eternal. Therefore, the promise of eternal life is more than the promise of eternal existence. Eternal existence seems to be granted to both believers and disbelievers. Thus, Scripture is in agreement with the logical argument that the intellect, because it is non-elemental, exists after the destruction of the elemental, or physical, body (*Promulgation* 415-16, *Some Answered Questions* 259-66).

Certain Scriptural passages suggest that some souls entering hell are eventually annihilated (Matt. 10:28). This may be because non-spiritual existence is non-existence in relation to spiritual existence (*Some Answered Questions* 319-20). 'Abdu'l-Bahá states, 'non-existence is only relative and absolute non-existence inconceivable' (*Promulgation* 88). More specifically, He writes:

> the torments of the other world, consist in being deprived of the special divine blessings and absolute bounties, and falling into the lowest degrees of existence. He who is deprived of these divine favors, although he continues after death, is considered as dead by the people of truth. (*Some Answered Questions* 261)

Eternal life, therefore, signifies the ever-enduring spiritual condition that characterizes the faithful believer. Attainment of spiritual perfections is what makes eternal life 'heavenly'.

## WHY RIGHTEOUSNESS ALONE IS INSUFFICIENT

Some Christians object to the view that attaining salvation, or heaven, is determined by our own spirituality and righteousness. They assert that Christ is the only way (John 14:6), that salvation is by grace through faith in Him (Eph. 2:8) 'not of works, lest anyone should boast' (Eph. 2:9). Some Christians maintain that their belief in salvation through grace is one of the primary distinctions between Christianity and other religions.[50] In other words,

---

50. This distinction does not appear to hold up to scrutiny. It is very likely that such views can be found at least among some adherents in all religions. See, e.g., the *Bhagavad-Gita*, which teaches that the eternal realm is reached by Krishna's grace (18:56, 18:63). See also A.C. Bhaktivedanta Swami Prabhupada's commentary, *Bhagavad-Gita As It Is* 825, 831. Some Christians may argue that Hindu views about grace are borrowed from Christianity but the Hindu view is equally supported by their Scriptures which are generally believed to pre-date the New Testament. In Islam it is believed that God rewards those who do good, but it is also accepted that forgiveness is not won by merit but flows from God's grace. See, e.g., Qur'án 57:21, 53: 32 and 39:53.

a righteous person simply does not have, nor can have, salvation if he or she does not accept Jesus.

The biblical verses that Christians use to support this view have a parallel in the Bahá'í writings. Bahá'u'lláh writes that our first duty is to recognize the Manifestation and 'whoso is deprived thereof, hath gone astray, *though he be the author of every righteous deed*' (*Synopsis and Codification* 11, emphasis added). But why must we believe in Christ, or any Manifestation, to attain salvation, if salvation is influenced by our righteous conduct? Why is righteous conduct not enough?

One answer is that both knowledge and deeds are necessary to humankind's spiritual progress, or salvation. 'Abdu'l-Bahá elaborates on this point in an explanation of Bahá'u'lláh's statement cited above:

> This blessed verse means that the foundation of success and salvation is the knowledge of God, and that results of the knowledge of God are the good actions which are the fruits of faith. (*Some Answered Questions* 275)

'Abdu'l-Bahá continues by explaining that those ignorant of the Manifestation or of God, but righteous in conduct, are not denied the pardon of God. Rather :

> If man has not this knowledge, he will be separated from God, and when this separation exists, good actions have not complete effect. (Ibid.)

'Abdu'l-Bahá is very clear about the importance of the knowledge of God:

> good actions alone, without the knowledge of God, cannot be the cause of eternal salvation, everlasting

success, and prosperity, and entrance into the kingdom. (*Some Answered Questions* 276)

Faith in God's Manifestations is essential to the acquisition of the knowledge of God. True rejection of a Manifestation is not the rejection of a name or title, but rather the rejection of a spiritual reality, 'the "Presence of God" Himself' (*Certitude* 143). If we see the perfections of Christ or Bahá'u'lláh, yet refuse to acknowledge and believe their truths, we have deprived ourselves of the guidance of God.

This point is seen in the Báb's statements to a certain Muslim who failed to recognize the Báb's station. The Báb writes:

> Hadst thou uttered 'yea' on hearing the Words of God, thou wouldst have been seen to have been worshipping God from the beginning that hath no beginning until the present day, never to have disobeyed Him, not even for the twinkling of an eye. Yet neither the upright deeds thou hast wrought during all thy life, nor the exertions thou didst make to banish every thought from thy heart save that of the good-pleasure of God, none of these did in truth profit thee, not even to the extent of a grain of mustard seed, inasmuch as thou didst veil thyself from God and tarried behind at the time of His manifestation. (*Selections from the Writings of the Báb* 31-2)

Later in the same tablet the Báb returns to this theme and compares righteousness and faith by pointing out to the Muslim who failed to recognize Him that the ultimate purpose of good deeds is the recognition of God:

> We are cognizant of thy righteous deeds, though they

shall avail thee nothing; for the whole object of such
righteousness is but recognition of God, thy Lord, and
undoubted faith in the Words revealed by Him.
(Ibid.)

The recognition of 'the Words revealed by Him' is essential.
For example, with the passage of time the Prophets abrogate
laws and practices that are no longer appropriate for
governing the affairs of humankind. Practices once thought
to be righteous may, in a later age, actually be detrimental to
humanity's spiritual development. Denying a new
Manifestation of God and insisting on following old laws in
the hope that such so-called righteousness will ensure
salvation is, in fact, denying the Source (i.e. the Manifestation) of the knowledge of God's law and will. This
knowledge is necessary for a correct spiritual life and a truly
harmonized state of being. It is impossible to imagine
heaven or a condition of salvation that is not in harmony
with God's will.

From these passages, and from 'Abdu'l-Bahá's statement
that 'results of the knowledge of God are the good actions
which are the fruits of faith' (*Some Answered Questions* 275),
an interrelatedness appears between faith in God's
Manifestations and righteousness. Faith in God's
Manifestations is conducive to righteousness and righteousness is conducive to faith (*Certitude* 192-200) and knowledge
of God. Bahá'u'lláh writes:

man's knowledge of God cannot develop fully and
adequately save by observing whatever hath been
ordained by Him and is set forth in His heavenly
Book. (*Tablets of Bahá'u'lláh* 268)

An important part of this equation between deeds and faith

also involves the role that a strong sense of religious faith plays in good conduct. The strength that comes from faith, devotion and prayer helps us to withstand tests, persevere after failures and remain steadfast in the face of difficulties.

## RESPONDING TO CHRISTIAN
## ARGUMENTS ABOUT ATONEMENT

**RESPONSES TO THE ARGUMENT THAT ONLY FAITH
IN CHRIST CAN BRING SALVATION**
We have seen that Christians believe salvation is by the grace
of God. This teaching is biblical (Eph. 2:8) and is also
expressed in the Bahá'í writings (*Certitude* 34). However,
most conservative Christians assert that the grace by which
we are saved can only come through faith in Christ - faith in
any other Manifestation, they assert, will not bring salvation.

From a Bahá'í point of view, the concept of grace held by
some Christians is too limited, but is the broader Bahá'í
concept of grace biblical? In fact, the Bible itself offers a very
lofty view of God's grace with such passages as:

the grace of God that brings salvation has appeared to
all men. (Titus 2:11)

That was the true Light [Christ] which gives light to
every man who comes into the world. (John 1:9)

In truth I [Peter] perceive that God shows no
partiality. But in every nation whoever fears Him and
works righteousness is accepted by Him. (Acts 10:35)

These verses are spoken within the historical context of the
Christian Revelation, but they all testify to God's love,

fairness and justice. Limiting these qualities solely to the relationship between God and Christians during the last two thousand years, is portraying a limited God.

The claims in the Scriptures that Jesus is the only way (John 14:6) refer to His reality as a Manifestation of God, the Word of God, that true Light, not exclusively to the physical person of Jesus or His name (apart from the fact that the name signifies the divine *reality*). It is the true Light of God that is the only 'way'. This Light is reflected perfectly through the historical Person of Jesus Christ and through all the Manifestations of God who have appeared throughout the world. Otherwise, in contradiction to Scripture, the 'grace of God that brings salvation' has not appeared to 'all men', and God would not be One Who shows 'no partiality'.

The fact that salvation is given by grace indicates God's love for humanity and His desire to save humankind from the consequences of sin. Such love is not consistent with the belief that God would create and then abandon the majority of the people of this world. It is inconceivable that God would be so unfair as to single out one group of people, give them the choice of belief and disbelief, but then leave most people without knowledge that guidance and a sure hope even existed.

It is a much more compelling and reasonable belief that a loving God would provide a means for all humankind to attain salvation. The evidence that this indeed He has done is found in the religions that exist all over the world.

## RESPONSES TO THE ARGUMENT THAT SALVATION IS ONLY MADE POSSIBLE BECAUSE OF THE SHEDDING OF JESUS' BLOOD

Another Christian objection to the Bahá'í point of view involves 'the shedding of blood' by Christ. If salvation is attainment to a spiritual state of being, as the result of following the Manifestation's teachings and example, why

does the Bible teach 'without the shedding of blood there is
no forgiveness of sins' (Heb. 9:22)? This is understood by
Christians to mean that if Christ had not died on the cross,
shedding his blood as a sacrificial offering to God, our sins
could not be forgiven. Thus, Christians assert, salvation is
linked specifically to Christ's atonement, not to our deeds.

The Bahá'í view maintains that the cross was a necessity
to establish an example of sacrifice in the world. This
example was intended to teach humanity that renunciation of
the world is essential to spiritual life. For this reason, Christ
submitted Himself to the cross and commanded the faithful
to follow His example:

> And he who does not take his cross and follow after
> me is not worthy of Me. (Matt. 10:38)

Without the powerful example of Jesus' sacrifice His
ultimate conviction in God's truth would not have been
manifest. People are motivated to renounce the sinful
attachment to worldly desires as a result of the love manifest
in the sacrifice of the Prophets. Their renunciation also
brings conviction to their words and to the idea that their
teachings are the path to eternal life. Today, the place of
Bahá'u'lláh's imprisonment, 'Akká, has the same symbolic
spiritual significance as the Cross. Bahá'u'lláh writes:

> We, verily, have come for your sakes, and have borne
> the misfortunes of the world for your salvation.
> (*Tablets of Bahá'u'lláh* 10)

and in another passage:

> My body hath endured imprisonment that ye may be
> released from the bondage of self. (Ibid.)

People are freed from the consequences of sin as a result of the powerful hold the example of the Manifestations has on their hearts. Believers who follow the Manifestation enter into a spiritual life characterized by a growing love of humanity, peace of mind, and happiness with what God has ordained in their lives. Moreover, they have arisen to leave sin behind and the anguish, despair and unhappiness that are its consequences. This guidance is established only because the Prophets persevere and suffer to bring about the conviction that their words are true. 'Abdu'l-Bahá explains the necessity of the shedding of blood in this way:

> There is no doubt that one who put forth such a claim as Christ announced would arouse the hostility of the world and be subjected to personal abuse. He realized that His blood would be shed and His body rent by violence. Notwithstanding His knowledge of what would befall Him, He arose to proclaim His message, suffered all tribulations and hardships from the people and finally offered His life as a sacrifice in order to illumine humanity - gave his blood in order to guide the world of mankind. He accepted every calamity and suffering in order to guide men to truth. Had He desired to save His own life, and were He without wish to offer Himself in sacrifice, He would not have been able to guide a single soul. There was no doubt that His blessed blood would be shed and His body broken. Nevertheless, that Holy Soul accepted calamity and death in His love for mankind. This is one of the meanings of sacrifice. (*Promulgation* 450)[51]

---

51. There are some doctrinal views that almost all Christians have in common. For instance, Protestants, Catholics and Eastern Orthodox Christians all accept and adhere to the belief that Christ had two natures: one human, one divine. However, the atonement has never crystallized into one accepted view, though most Protestant Fundamentalists are in general agreement with regard to their basic views about atonement. Historically, a great many viewpoints have existed, and individuals such as Origen (c 185-c.254), Anselm of Canterbury (c.1033-1109), and Thomas

Thus, from the Bahá'í point of view, the shedding of blood is indeed necessary to atonement, not because of its superiority to the sacrifices endured by the other Prophets but because it testifies to the truth of God.

## RESPONSES TO THE ASSERTION THAT ONLY THE SACRIFICE OF JESUS CAN ATONE FOR HUMANKIND'S SINS

Some Christians object to the Bahá'í view of Jesus' sacrifice because they believe His sacrifice is unique. They assert that Jesus is the only acceptable sacrifice for the redemption of humankind because of His sinlessness. He is the only one without blemish, perfect, the best there is to offer. Only Jesus is perfect because He was born of the Virgin Mary and avoided the guilt of Adam's sin. This view involves a concept often referred to as 'original sin'.

Some Christians argue that Paul teaches the concept of original sin. The following verse is often quoted in support of this doctrine:

For as in Adam all die, even so in Christ all shall be made alive. (1 Cor. 15:22)

Bahá'ís do not believe this view (i.e., the doctrine of original sin) to be biblical. 'Abdu'l-Bahá explains the meaning of Paul's words as follows:

The Christ is the central point of the Holy Spirit: He is born of the Holy Spirit; He is raised up by the Holy

Aquinas (1224-74) have all contributed different ideas. 'Abdu'l-Bahá's statement that Christ gave 'His blood in order to guide the world of mankind' (*Promulgation* 450) suggests some similarity to the view often associated with the Christian philosopher and theologian Peter Abelard (1079-1142). Abelard emphasized the importance of the death of Christ as an example which brought salvation through the spiritual influence it has on people's hearts. (See *The Christian Understanding of Atonement* 324-8). This rationalistic view is considered inadequate by some conservative Christians. (See Barackman's *Practical Christian Theology* 120.)

Spirit; He is the descendant of the Holy Spirit. That is to say, that the reality of Christ does not descend from Adam; no, it is born of the Holy Spirit. Therefore, this verse in Corinthians, 'As in Adam all die even so in Christ shall all be made alive', means, according to this terminology, that Adam is the father of man, that is to say, he is the cause of the physical life of mankind; his was a physical fatherhood. He is a living soul, but he is not the giver of spiritual life. Whereas Christ is the cause of the spiritual life of man, and with regard to the spirit his was the spiritual fatherhood. Adam is a living soul, Christ is a quickening spirit. (*Some Answered Questions* 135)

'Abdu'l-Bahá explains that what is inherited from Adam is not Adam's sin or guilt but, rather, the physical nature that tempts humankind towards sin. This truth is suggested in James' words:

But each one is tempted when he is drawn by his own desires and enticed. Then, when desire has conceived, it gives birth to sin; and sin, when it is full grown, brings forth death. (James 1:15)

'Abdu'l-Bahá states:

Adam was the cause of physical life, and as the physical world of man is the world of imperfections, and imperfections are the equivalent of death, Paul compared the physical imperfections to death. (*Some Answered Questions* 136)

From the Bahá'í point of view, people do not inherit the sin of Adam or the guilt of anyone's sin. They only inherit a physical nature which, if not controlled, can compel them to sin.

The Christian argument also implies that God punishes men for the sins of others, but the Bible itself gives us reason to doubt this belief:

> The soul who sins shall die. The son shall not bear the guilt of the father, nor the father bear the guilt of the son. The righteousness of the righteous shall be upon himself, and the wickedness of the wicked shall be upon himself. (Ezek. 18:20)

'Abdu'l-Bahá addresses the issue with this explanation:

> They [Christians] say that Adam disobeyed the command of God and partook of the fruit of the forbidden tree, thereby committing a sin which was transmitted as a heritage to His posterity. They teach that because of Adam's sin all His descendants have, likewise, committed transgression and have become responsible through inheritance; that, consequently, all mankind deserves punishment and must make retribution; and that God sent forth His son as a sacrifice in order that man might be forgiven and the human race delivered from the consequences of Adam's transgression. We wish to consider these statements from the standpoint of reason. Could we conceive of the Divinity, Who is Justice itself, inflicting punishment upon the posterity of Adam for Adam's own sin and disobedience? Even if we should see a governor, an earthly ruler, punishing a son for the wrong-doing of his father, we would look upon that ruler as an unjust man. Granted the father committed a wrong, what was the wrong committed by the son? There is no connection between the two,

Adam's sin was not the sin of His posterity, especially
as Adam is a thousand generations back of the man
today. (*Promulgation* 449)

'Abdu'l-Bahá rejects the idea that people are guilty of Adam's
sin because it would be contrary to God's justice. Our own
guilt is the result of our own sin. Jesus was perfect not
because He avoided Adam's sin through His parentage, but
because He personally chose not to sin - this is the basis of his
sinlessness. Moreover, Adam was created without inherited
sin, yet he eventually disobeyed God and sinned. Being born
without sin gave no immunity to it.

Proof of Jesus' perfection cannot be determined by the
Virgin Birth; it must be determined by the testimony of
Scripture and by what is known of His life and teachings.
Relying only on the available knowledge of His life creates
some difficulty, since not much is actually known. This
approach is applicable to all Manifestations of God.
Perfection can only be proven by our knowledge of the
Manifestations. Since our knowledge is not complete,
absolute perfection cannot be determined absolutely but must
be trusted as a probable fact. In this case, the basis of faith is
what we know from the testimony of Scripture.[52]

Bahá'ís believe all Manifestations of God are 'pure from
every sin, and sanctified from faults' (*Some Answered
Questions* 119-21) and possess all the perfections of divinity
(*Certitude* 104). The sacrifices of all Manifestations are
acceptable to God, all are qualified to act as humankind's
Guides for Salvation and an examination of their lives and
their teachings backs this up.

52. Faith, as opposed to blind faith, as understood and intended by this writer, is generally a
rational inductive process. An act of faith is an act of trust in some probability established by
consciously or subconsciously known evidence. However, this type of faith is distinguishable
from the goal of faith itself, which is certitude, and which can be attained through the actual
experience of the divine by directly following the teachings of God in one's personal life. Faith,
in other words, is verified in the religious experience itself.

## ARE BAHÁ'ÍS 'SAVED'?

What, then, if a Christian should ask 'are we saved?' In the opinion of this writer, the answer is 'yes', for even though our spiritual life is a progressing condition, we have nevertheless 'entered into the life of faith - the heavenly and everlasting life' (*Certitude* 114). Furthermore, according to the Bahá'í view, salvation is not a condition that we await at the end of our physical lives. It begins here and now - and its evidence and benefits also manifest themselves in the here and now. Nor is there any doubt that Bahá'u'lláh is Lord and Saviour, for His teachings, perfections and claims all testify to this truth. Bahá'u'lláh writes:

> Fix your gaze upon Him Who is the Temple of God[53]
> amongst men. He, in truth, hath offered up his life as
> a ransom for the redemption of the world. He verily,
> is the All-Bountiful, the Gracious, the Most High.
> (*Gleanings* 315)

One distinguishing aspect of Bahá'u'lláh's message of redemption is that He has taken the eternal truths of God and applied them more to humanity as a whole than to the individual believers (*Promised Day* 119-20). Circumstances were radically different in the world prior to the appearance of Bahá'u'lláh and the type of broader co-operation between people which He teaches was not possible in the age of Christ (*Promised Day* 119).

However, even though the central teachings of the Bahá'í Faith focus on 'the regeneration of the whole world' (*Gleanings* 243), Bahá'u'lláh's message is also concerned with

---

53. It may be significant that Bahá'u'lláh refers to Himself as the Temple of God in this context, because the Temple is the place where sacrificial offerings were made to God for the atonement of the people. (See, e.g., Lev. 16). It was also the place where the Law of God (brought down from Mount Sinai by Moses) was kept and which signified the presence of God on earth.

the individual believer and his or her relationship with God. This is especially evident in His writings, such as *The Hidden Words* and His prayers and meditations.

**BIBLICAL REFERENCES FOR PART THREE**
For future reference, many of the verses used in Part Three's explanations are listed below. It may also be useful to read through these chapters again and make an outline of those verses that Christians use in their explanations, since familiarity with the ones they emphasize is always helpful. The more we are able to refer to the Bible, the less we will have to rely on our own or on somebody else's paraphrased version of God's Revelation.

God's grace is all-embracing:
Titus 2:11
John 1:9
Acts 10:35
Both faith and deeds are important to salvation:
Rom. 2:7
Rom. 3:31
Rom. 6:15
1 John 3:6
James 2:26
The significance of Christ's death on the cross concerns Christ's example:
Matt. 10:38
Concerning original sin:
Ezek. 18:20
Nature of heaven and hell:
in this section John 3:15, Matt. 18:8, Rev. 20:10, and Matt. 10:28 were noted. However you may find it best to simply refer to verses most frequently employed by 'Abdu'l-Bahá, which are: John 3:13

and Matt. 8:22 or Luke 9:60. John 3:13 suggests
the non-material, non-geographical nature of
heaven. Matt. 8:22 suggests the non-physical
nature of eternal life.

It is important to study the explanations, since the meanings
of the verses are not always self-evident, but can be used as
supporting testimony. For example, Ezekiel 18:20 does not
deny original sin, it simply suggests the injustice implied by
the doctrine of original sin.

In many cases, as demonstrated in this section, there are
great similarities between the verses of the Bible and the
Bahá'í writings. The distinctions involve differences of
interpretation. The areas of disagreement primarily centre
around the Christian accusation that all other religions rely
solely on good works, that the individual faith of non-
Christians is invalid since it is not based on the particular
Person of Jesus, and the assertion that only the acceptance of
Christ can ensure eternal life. Resolution of these
disagreements can sometimes involve a very broad discussion
of grace, salvation, righteousness, faith, heaven and hell, the
proofs of other Manifestations, and so on, rather than
references to the Bible, which Christians do not emphasize
when speaking of atonement.

In Part 2 we learned that many Christians believe that Christ
is God and therefore, they argue, He is uniquely different
from, and superior to, the Founders of the other world
religions. In Part 3 we learned that Christians also believe
that Christ is unique and superior to the Founders of the
other world religions with regard to salvation and atonement.
In the next section we will respond to yet another Christian
doctrine that many Christians believe elevates Christianity
above other world religions; that is; they believe the Founders

of the other religions, for example, Buddha, Muhammad and even Bahá'u'lláh, all died and were buried, whereas Jesus was resurrected physically from the dead.

*part four*

## THE RESURRECTION OF CHRIST

### INTRODUCTION

The resurrection of Jesus Christ is often viewed by Christians as proof of His Divinity. Some Christians also believe that the resurrection is evidence that Jesus has the power to, and will, save those who believe in Him from death (i.e., physical death). They argue that since Jesus rose from the dead literally, when He returns to establish His kingdom on earth He will have the power to raise from the dead Christians who have died in the past. At that time, they believe, He will end physical death completely so that all will live eternally in His kingdom.

These views are based on the literal interpretation of certain verses in the Bible that we will look at more closely in the next chapter. We will specifically focus on conservative Christian beliefs and Bahá'í explanations about Jesus' resurrection and, in Chapter 12, we will respond to specific Christian arguments against symbolic interpretations of the resurrection.

# 11

## THE MEANING OF RESURRECTION

### CHRISTIAN BELIEFS CONCERNING THE RESURRECTION OF JESUS: WHY A PHYSICAL RESURRECTION IS IMPORTANT TO CHRISTIANS

Some Christians, especially the more conservative ones, insist that the resurrection of Jesus Christ was a literal, physical, event. They believe that the actual physical body of Jesus literally arose from the dead and ascended into heaven - the sky we see above our heads as we stand on the earth. Since Jesus was able to do this He must be God, since only God has the power to overcome death.

However, the main significance of the resurrection to conservative Christians is its proof that Jesus has the power to restore life to our physical bodies and so give us eternal life. To refute the physical resurrection is, to such Christians, to refute the evidence that Jesus has the power to overcome death. Some Christians believe that since the Bible depicts Jesus' resurrection so clearly as a physical event it would be a terrible and heartless hoax perpetrated against humanity if it were not, in fact, literally true.

### POINTS OF AGREEMENT: BAHÁ'Í TEACHINGS ABOUT THE RESURRECTION

The Bahá'í Faith agrees both that the resurrection happened and that without it Christianity, indeed all religion, would be futile. 'Abdu'l-Bahá insists that the resurrection is a 'fact', but it is a 'spiritual and divine fact' not an 'outward fact' (*Some*

*Answered Questions*, ch. 23). This conviction does not, however, necessitate, depend upon, or assert that the resurrection is a physical event. The Bahá'í belief is that the Biblical account of the resurrection is symbolic of an important and essential spiritual transformation brought about by Jesus Christ. This transformation occurs in every dispensation as a result of the Revelation of God. Christians have simply chosen to read Scripture literally.

## 'ABDU'L-BAHÁ'S EXPLANATION OF THE RESURRECTION

According to the teachings of 'Abdu'l-Bahá, the 'resurrections of the Divine Manifestations are not of the body' (*Some Answered Questions*, ch. 23). 'Abdu'l-Bahá states that the resurrection has 'a spiritual and divine signification', and has 'no connection with material things' (*Some Answered Questions*, ch. 23). More specifically, He explains the symbolic meaning as follows:

> the disciples were troubled and agitated after the martyrdom of Christ. The Reality of Christ, which signifies His teachings, His bounties, His perfections, and His spiritual power, was hidden and concealed for two or three days after His martyrdom, and was not resplendent and manifest. No, rather it was lost; for the believers were few in number and were troubled and agitated. The Cause of Christ was like a lifeless body; and, when after three days the disciples became assured and steadfast, and began to serve the Cause of Christ, and resolved to spread the divine teachings, putting His counsels into practice, and arising to serve Him, the Reality of Christ became resplendent and his bounty appeared; His religion found life, His teachings and His admonitions became evident and visible. In

other words, the Cause of Christ was like a lifeless body, until the life and the bounty of the Holy Spirit surrounded it. (*Some Answered Questions*, ch. 23)

In this explanation 'Abdu'l-Bahá indicates that the raising of the body of Christ was actually the coming to life of Christ's teachings in the disciples, the restoration of their belief and conviction.

The resurrection was the most appropriate symbol that the Apostles could have used to affirm that the physical death of Jesus was not, as the Jews believed, evidence that Jesus was not the Messiah. The Jews rejected Jesus' claim to be the Messiah because this claim implied Lordship. His death on the cross was for them the final evidence disproving His Lordship: He was powerless to defeat His enemies. The Jews failed to perceive the meaning of true 'life' and true sovereignty. To Jesus, true life was the life of the spirit not the flesh (John 6:63). Life symbolized the condition of belief, the life of faith, and the path to eternal life was faith in Jesus. Unbelief was symbolized by death, even as Jesus indicated when He said, 'Follow Me, and let the dead bury their own dead' (Matt. 8:22).

The resurrection was a symbol, in keeping with Christ's own use of terminology, which asserted that He lived on. It meant that His place in the hearts of the believers is what imparted true life. For the Pharisees, the crucifixion meant that Jesus was finished, His claims disproven, but the Apostles countered their objections with the startling assertion that Jesus was alive! What the Apostles conveyed to the world in symbolic language was the reality that Christ, 'is ever-living, everlasting, eternal. For that divine reality there is no beginning, no ending, and therefore, *there can be no death*' (*Promulgation* 395, emphasis added). The resurrection was a powerful way to symbolize and proclaim this great truth.

## THE HEAVEN THAT CHRIST ASCENDED TO

It is not difficult to see how 'Abdu'l-Bahá's explanation is consistent with the accounts given in the Bible. According to the Bible, Jesus was taken up into heaven:

> Now when He had spoken these things, while they watched, He was taken up, and a cloud received Him out of their sight. (Acts 1:9)

This account sounds very literal, and continues with the words 'they looked steadfastly towards heaven as He went up' (Acts 1:10). But what does 'heaven' mean? Is it literally the sky above the earth or does Scripture indicate another meaning? 'Abdu'l-Bahá says it does have another meaning. He points out that Jesus Himself stated the following:

> No one has ascended to heaven but He who came down from heaven that is, the Son of Man who is in heaven. (John 3:13; *Some Answered Questions* 119)

In this statement Jesus says He is in heaven, even though He stands on the earth. In another passage, Jesus states:

> For I have come down from heaven not to do My own will, but the will of Him who sent Me. (John 6:38; *Some Answered Questions* 119)

When Jesus said this, Scripture records that He received this reaction:

> The Jews then murmured against Him, because He said, 'I am the bread which came down from heaven.' And they said, 'Is not this Jesus, the son of Joseph, whose father and mother we know? How is

it then that He says, 'I have come down from heaven"? (John 6:41-2)

'Abdu'l-Bahá explains:

> Notice also that it is said that Christ came from heaven, though he came from the womb of Mary, and His body was born of Mary. It is clear, then, that when it is said that the Son of man is come from heaven, this has not an outward but an inward signification; it is a spiritual, not a material, fact. The meaning is that though, apparently, Christ was born from the womb of Mary, in reality He came from heaven, from the center of the Sun of Reality, from the Divine World, and the Spiritual Kingdom . . . likewise His ascension to heaven is a spiritual and not material ascension. (*Some Answered Questions* 119-20)

From the Bahá'í point of view, heaven has a spiritual not a material meaning. The ascension of Christ into heaven, therefore, cannot reasonably be to the material heaven above the physical earth.

## THE RISEN BODY SYMBOLIZES THE CHRISTIAN CHURCH

'Abdu'l-Bahá, as was noted earlier, has equated the risen body of Christ to the faith of the disciples after His crucifixion. We can examine where this equation is indicated in the Scriptures. Paul frequently refers to the believers as the body of Christ:

> We, being many, are one body in Christ, and individually members of one another. (Rom. 12:5)

And He is the Head of the body, the Church. (Col.
1:18)

These verses show that Paul also equated the believers, that is,
the Church, with the body of Christ. 'Abdu'l-Bahá pointed
out that after the crucifixion of Jesus the disciples, i.e. those
who were the representatives of the Church, were like a lifeless
body, 'troubled and agitated' rather than 'assured and steadfast'
(*Some Answered Questions* 120). When the Apostles became
assured and steadfast they brought life back into the Church or,
symbolically, into the body of Christ. Notice how similar this
idea is to Paul's own words, for Paul compares the past 'when
we were dead in trespasses' with the present when God 'made
us alive together with Christ' (Eph. 2:5). Paul even goes on to
say that they had been 'raised' up 'to sit together in the
heavenly places in Christ Jesus' (Eph. 2:6):

> Even when we were dead in trespasses, [God] made us
> alive together with Christ (by grace you have been
> saved), and raised us up together, and made us sit
> together in the heavenly places in Christ Jesus. (Eph.
> 2:5-6)

This idea is evident in many other passages:

> For as the body is one and has many members, but all
> the members of that one body, being many, are one
> body, so also is Christ. For by one Spirit we were all
> baptized into one body. (1 Cor. 12:12-13)

> There should be no schism in the body. (1 Cor. 12:25)

> Now you are the body of Christ, and members
> individually. (1 Cor. 12:27)

For we are members of His body, and His flesh and of His bones. (Eph. 5:29-30)

Paul even refers to the believers as being 'of His flesh and of His bones'(Eph. 5:29-30). These verses suggest that the flesh and bones of Jesus, His risen body, are actually symbolic of the Church - its spiritual and heavenly reality.

In the next chapter we will examine the consistency of 'Abdu'l-Bahá's explanation with the accounts of Jesus' appearances to the Apostles after His Crucifixion.

# 12

## RESPONDING TO CHRISTIAN ARGUMENTS AGAINST THE SPIRITUAL INTERPRETATION OF THE RESURRECTION

### INTRODUCTION

Despite the plausibility of the Bahá'í explanation, some Christians are often very adamant that the resurrection is meant to be taken literally. The following five arguments do not contain all the points some Christians list, but they do cover what some Christians consider to be the most forceful arguments against the belief in the spiritual resurrection.[54] For the purpose of this study these arguments are categorized as: (1) The Empty Tomb Argument, (2) The Flesh and Bones Argument, (3) The Doubting Thomas Argument, (4) The Many Witnesses Argument, and (5) The Terrible Hoax Argument.

Apart from the 'Empty Tomb Argument', all of these involve accounts of Jesus' appearances after His resurrection. Some scholars argue that these accounts were added later and are not authentic. This view rests upon a variety of assumptions about certain early manuscripts and about characteristics of the language used in manuscripts. Most conservative Christians reject the assumptions and conclusions of scholars who challenge the authenticity of the accounts in the Bible.

The debate over the post-resurrection narratives raises the question of whether Bahá'ís should attempt to discern

54. See *The Resurrection Factor* by Josh McDowell.

symbolic meanings behind accounts that some scholars assert are not even authentic. A statement written by the Guardian helps answer this question:

> We do not believe that there was a bodily resurrection after the crucifixion of Christ, but that there was a time after His ascension when His disciples perceived spiritually His true greatness and realized He was eternal in being. This is what has been reported symbolically in the New Testament and been misunderstood. His eating with His disciples after resurrection is the same thing. (*Lights of Guidance* 368)

Since the Guardian indicates that the New Testament reports use symbolic language to convey a message consistent with Bahá'í teachings, it follows that these accounts are inspired of God even as is the rest of the Gospel. In the following responses to Christian arguments, we will attempt to understand the symbolism in these accounts.

## RESPONSES TO THE EMPTY TOMB ARGUMENT

If the body of Jesus did not rise physically, how can the empty tomb be explained? The Gospel unmistakably indicates that the body disappeared from the tomb, despite the large stone and a Roman guard.[55]

Bahá'u'lláh indicated that the term 'tomb' is used in Scripture symbolically (*Certitude* 119-20). The Guardian also states that the scriptural word 'tomb' can have an allegorical significance meaning the 'tomb of unbelief' (*Lights of Guidance* 358). Using this definition, the accounts in the Gospel can be interpreted as meaning that because of the

---

55. It is perhaps worth noting that even if the accounts of the empty tomb, given in the narratives of the Gospel, are taken literally they do not indicate that Jesus physically rose from the dead. An empty tomb is not in itself proof that the body placed in it has risen from the dead.

doubts of the Apostles, the spirit of Christ, His teachings and His cause were lifeless, in the tomb of unbelief. This explanation suggests additional consistency between the Gospel and 'Abdu'l-Bahá's explanation concerning the disciples' relationship to the meaning of the resurrection.

A possible explanation for the specific detail of the stone in front of the tomb is that it represents the doubt of the Apostles that resulted from Jesus' death on the cross. That is, the stone symbolized what Paul calls the 'stumbling block' of Jesus' death on the cross (1 Cor. 1:18-24). The angels could symbolize those who arose to dispel the doubts (i.e., moved the stone of doubt from the tomb), and the Roman guard could be symbolic of the reason for the doubts. That is, people expected the Messiah to dispel the Roman oppression, but the power of Rome seemed entirely unshaken, remaining a threat to the future of the Church. The fleeing of the guard (or as the Gospel of Matthew indicates, the guard 'became like dead men' Matt. 28:4) could mean that, although Rome had not yet been conquered and the physical body of Jesus had been crucified, the world had not, and could not, destroy His Spirit and prevent the establishment of His Cause. With this realization, the Roman soldiers were no longer an obstacle to Christian belief, and the stumbling block of Jesus' death was rolled back, freeing their faith from the tomb of doubt and unbelief.

If the account is symbolic, then it must be admitted that it is not possible to know for sure what happened to the actual body of Jesus. The fate of the faith of the disciples is the point of the story, not the physical body of Jesus. However, if we speculate, and on this matter there can only be speculation, there are some points in the Gospel that may suggest the actual fate of the physical body. The Gospel states that Jesus prophesied He would rise after three days. The Jewish authorities wanted to do everything they could to prevent anyone from asserting that this prophecy had been fulfilled literally. This is apparent from the fact that the Jewish priests appealed to the Roman leader Pilate to place a guard by the tomb to prevent the disciples stealing the body and proclaiming a miracle. (Matt. 27:62-4)

Let us assume this effort made by the priests is literal rather than symbolic of their futility in trying to defeat Christianity. Let us also assume that the tomb and the stone are literal. Even if we make these assumptions, a plausible explanation is apparent. The angels, or devoted souls who moved the stone, would likely have realized that the authorities, who viewed Jesus' words from a literal point of view, had only one way to prove that the body of Jesus had not resurrected physically: that was to re-open the tomb after three days had passed and bring out the body. In this way the priests could claim the prophecy had not been fulfilled. If the tomb was re-opened by the Jews and Romans, Jesus' body would be exposed to further, and perhaps worse, desecration.

Consequently, there existed a very strong motive for the early Christians to remove the body as soon as possible. This is, of course, only speculation and cannot be verified. The accounts probably do not pertain to such outward events but, nevertheless, the opponents of Christ hoped they could defeat Him and prevent the establishment of the Church. The resurrection accounts symbolize their failure to accomplish either of these goals.

**RESPONSES TO THE FLESH AND BONES ARGUMENT**
According to the Gospel of Luke the following account is given of Jesus' appearance to the Apostles after the crucifixion:

> Now as they said these things, Jesus Himself stood in the midst of them,'Peace to you.' But they were

terrified and frightened, and supposed they had seen a
spirit. And He said to them, 'Why are you troubled?
And why do doubts arise in your hearts? Behold My
hands and My feet, that it is I myself. Handle Me and
see, for a spirit does not have flesh and bones as you
see I have.' When He had said this, He showed them
His hands and His feet. But while they still did not
believe for joy, and marveled, He said to them, 'Have
you any food here?' So they gave Him a piece of a
broiled fish and some honeycomb. And He took it
and ate in their presence . . . And He opened their
understanding, that they might comprehend the
Scriptures. (Luke 24:36-45)

In these verses Christ says 'a spirit does not have flesh and
bones as you see I have'. The word 'spirit' does not have
here a benevolent and positive connotation, as suggested by
the statement that the disciples 'were terrified and
frightened, and supposed they had seen a spirit'. They
thought they had seen something threatening with a
negative consequence or reality. If we understand that the
resurrected Christ is symbolic of Christ's continuing
influence, or the living Church and its believers raised from
the death of disbelief, then there is reason for the Apostles
to be frightened.

The Apostles were the close companions and recognized
associates of Christ and were naturally seen as the remaining
leaders of His Cause. Jesus had provoked the opposition of
the authorities to such an extent that they sought to kill Him,
and He was crucified. If the Apostles realized that the Cause
of Jesus was not destroyed by the crucifixion - that people
were still arising to proclaim and follow His teachings - then
they would likely have been afraid for their lives. After all,
when Jesus was arrested, the Apostles 'forsook Him and fled'

(Matt. 26:56). Peter even denied knowing Him three times in order to save himself (Matt. 26:69-75).

So when the Apostles saw that Christianity was alive they first feared for their lives. But then they came to realize that the Cause of Jesus (symbolized by the term 'spirit') should not frighten them, for the Cause (spirit) of Jesus had qualities (symbolized as the flesh and bones) uncharacteristic of a 'spirit' that should be feared. Rather than be frightened that the continuance and existence of the living body of Christ, the Church, might lead to their own martyrdom, they accepted and believed it as a Cause worth dying for. As Christ taught, 'he who loses his life for My sake will find it' (Matt. 10:39). Realizing and accepting this, they gave up their fears and became steadfast.

Hence, Paul calls the believers the 'flesh' and 'bones' of Christ (Eph.5:29-30). The believers are the Church and the Church is the body of Christ - 'His flesh' and 'His bones' (Eph. 5:29). Therefore, when the Apostles saw the signs and evidence of Christ as the risen Lord, they were actually seeing the living spirit of the believers who made up the Church.

The account continues with these words:

> But while they still did not believe for joy, and marveled, He said to them, 'Have you any food here?' So they gave Him a piece of a broiled fish and some honeycomb. And He took it and ate in their presence (Luke 24:41-42).

The giving of food to Christ can be understood as representing the giving of spiritual guidance, by the Apostles, to the believers or Church, representing the body of Christ. It can also be seen as the Apostles assuming their rightful roles as the leaders and guides of the Church.

This is one explanation that is a further application of 'Abdu'l-Bahá's equation of the risen body of Christ with the Church.

## RESPONSES TO THE DOUBTING THOMAS ARGUMENT

This argument is also put forward in support of a literal interpretation of the appearances of Christ on the grounds that the literal recordings are so clear that they preclude any other interpretation. However, 'Abdu'l-Bahá's explanation can be consistently applied to the texts. If we look at this account of doubting Thomas symbolically, it reveals that the risen Christ is, once again, the re-awakened believers and the establishment of the Church:

> But Thomas, called Didymus, one of the twelve, was not with them when Jesus came. The other disciples therefore said to him, 'We have seen the Lord.' But he said to them, 'Unless I see in His hands the print of the nails, and put my finger into the print of the nails, and put my hand into His side, I will not believe.' And after eight days His disciples were again inside, and Thomas with them. Jesus came, the doors being shut, and stood in the midst, and said, 'Peace to you.' Then He said to Thomas, 'Reach your finger here, and look at My hands; and reach your hand here, and put it into My side. Do not be unbelieving, but believing.' And Thomas answered and said to Him, 'My Lord and my God.' Jesus said to him, 'Thomas, because you have seen Me, you have believed. Blessed are those who have not seen and yet have believed.' (John 20:24-9)

There are several indications that this passage, like the others, has a very reasonable explanation. If we once again apply to this account the belief that the risen Christ is the re-awakened believers, then the meaning is as follows: The Apostles have told Thomas that Christ is alive in the hearts of the believers and lives on in the Church; and the Church has been established even though Christ has been crucified; and they have seen the evidence of this truth, and are therefore asking him to give up his doubts, acknowledge this truth, and re-commit his life to Christ.

Thomas, however, maintains that he does not believe that the Cause of Christ is still living amongst them. He then asserts that only when he sees the signs of Christ's suffering, (i.e., the nail prints and spear wound), will he accept that Jesus is risen. That is, these signs, which are the evidence of Jesus' suffering and of His willingness to die for humanity, must also characterize the Church. Thomas is therefore saying: only when he sees the believers willing to die and suffer for Christ will he believe that the Church is indeed risen and living.

When Christ appears to Thomas and reveals these signs, it is symbolic of Thomas having seen the evidence of the Church, the believers' willingness to suffer and endure persecution for the love of Christ. For this reason Thomas believes. The Gospel then goes on to teach that those who believe, even though they do not see others willing to suffer for the Faith, are blessed. Their faith, unlike Thomas', is not dependent on the actions of others.

Once again, we can see that 'Abdu'l-Bahá's teachings are applicable to the actual text and reveal the great spiritual truth of the Gospel. The spiritual message of the texts itself testifies that the post-resurrection narrative is inspired of God and should be appreciated for the guidance and assurance it imparts to us.

### RESPONSES TO THE MANY WITNESSES ARGUMENT
The Many Witnesses Argument proposes that the Gospel and the Epistles repeatedly refer to numerous individuals who see

Christ after the crucifixion. There is Jesus' appearance to a multitude of 500 believers (1 Cor. 15:6), the appearance to the Emmaus disciples (Luke 24:13-33), to the women returning from the tomb (Matt. 28:9-10), to Stephen (Acts 7:55), and to John on Patmos (Rev. 1:10-19).

All the witnesses are believers, however, and none of the verses indicate conclusively that the appearance of Christ is meant to be understood literally as the resurrection of His physical body. Are they witnesses to the reawakening of the Church: 'He is the Head of the body, the Church' (Col. 1:18), or are they witnesses to the appearance of the physical body of Jesus? There are no outside accounts from non-believers who saw a resurrected body that they identified as Jesus, nor any account which, when viewed symbolically, does not suggest a plausible spiritual significance.

Paul says the resurrected Christ appeared to him last (1 Cor. 15). However, the accounts of the appearance of Christ to Paul, recorded in Acts (chs 9, 22, 26) seem to be descriptions of a vision. In one instance, while he was in a trance praying, he describes hearing Christ (Acts 22:17-21). Perhaps the most significant factor here is that in all the accounts of Christ's appearance to Paul on the road to Damascus, Christ asks Paul: 'why are you persecuting Me?' (Acts 9:4, 22:7, 26:12). Yet we know Paul is not seeking to persecute Christ, who has already been crucified but, rather, His followers, the 'disciples of the Lord' (Acts 9:1). Why then does the risen Christ say to Paul, 'why are you persecuting Me?' if the risen Christ is not actually the living Church? Not surprisingly, it is Paul who continually equates the living body of Christ with the Church.

## RESPONSES TO THE TERRIBLE HOAX ARGUMENT
The 'Terrible Hoax Argument' is simply that, if the resurrection is not literal, the Apostles must either have been

the victims of a hoax or be conspirators in perpetrating a hoax upon humanity. Some Christians assert that whoever denies the physical resurrection is implying such a hoax. That the Scriptures should be intentionally deceptive is impossible, so Christians conclude that the literal interpretation of the resurrection must be true. If the resurrection were symbolic, the Apostles would have said so, they argue.

From a Bahá'í point of view, no lie, hoax or conspiracy is contained in the Scriptures. Understanding why the Apostles preached that Christ had risen, knowing full well that it was not a physical event, presents no difficulty. We must reflect on Christ's manner of speech throughout His ministry. If it is deception to use words and phrases with literal meanings to convey spiritual messages, how are we to understand Christ's words that 'unless one is born again, he cannot see the kingdom of God' (John 3:3) or this phrase: 'unless you eat the flesh of the Son of Man and drink His blood, you have no life in you'? (John 6:53). When the Apostles preached that Christ had risen, they were speaking as Christ Himself had spoken. The use of symbols is necessary to convey truths that cannot be conveyed by ordinary speech. The symbolic language of Scripture is also God's way of testing the hearts of His servants (*Certitude* 49 and 255. See also Heb. 4:12).

## CONCLUSION: THE BAHÁ'Í FAITH AFFIRMS THE SPIRITUAL RESURRECTION OF CHRIST

As Bahá'ís, we should be very careful to prevent our explanations from giving the impression that the Bahá'í Faith does not teach the truth of the resurrection. 'Abdu'l-Bahá states:

> When the truth of this subject becomes clear, and the symbol is explained, science in no way contradicts it;

but, on the contrary, science and intelligence affirm
it. (*Some Answered Questions* 121)

Our purpose is not to reject the resurrection, but rather to
'affirm it'. The Bahá'í view, however, is that this affirmation
should be in accordance with both science and Scripture.
'Abdu'l-Bahá states:

> Besides these explanations, it has been established and
> proved by science that the visible heaven is a limitless
> area, void and empty, where innumerable stars and
> planets revolve. (*Some Answered Questions* 120)

In other words, a physical ascension of Christ into heaven is
not logical in the light of clearly established scientific
knowledge. The Bahá'í view contradicts neither science nor
Scripture. Paul stresses the importance of the resurrection of
Christ in these words:

> And if Christ is not risen, then our preaching is vain
> and your faith is also vain. (1 Cor. 15:14)

Throughout chapter 15 of I Corinthians Paul elaborates on
the importance and necessity of the resurrection. Bahá'ís
believe the risen Christ is the re-awakening and spiritualizing
influence of His Spirit among the believers. Without this re-
awakening, preaching is indeed vain and faith is also vain.
Bahá'u'lláh writes:

> is not the object of every Revelation to effect a
> transformation in the whole character of mankind, a
> transformation that shall manifest itself both
> outwardly and inwardly, that shall affect both its inner
> life and external condition? For if the character of

mankind be not changed, the futility of God's universal Manifestations would be apparent. (*Certitude* 240-1)

Therefore, while it is true that the Bahá'í Faith views the resurrection as symbolic of a spiritual reality, the central importance of the resurrection remains primary and essential. The resurrection symbolizes the change in our lives that the Manifestations have come into the world to accomplish.

It is also very significant that Paul himself states the following in this same chapter of 1 Corinthians:

So also is the resurrection of the dead. The body is sown in corruption, it is raised in incorruption. It is sown in dishonour, it is raised in glory. It is sown in weakness, it is raised in power. It is sown a natural body, it is raised a spiritual body. There is a natural body, and there is a spiritual body. (1 Cor. 15:42-4)

These statements add weight to the Bahá'í interpretation. Paul points out, 'it is raised a spiritual body'. Some Christians, nevertheless, insist that the resurrection must be literal, and that 'spiritual body' must mean a physical body no longer subject to the normal conditions of disease and decomposition; the conditions that were consequences of Adam's original sin. But Paul continues his discourse thus:

Now this I say, brethren, that flesh and blood cannot inherit the kingdom of God; nor does corruption inherit incorruption. (1 Cor. 15:50)

This verse suggests that the resurrection is not about literal 'flesh and blood'. The risen body of the Church is made spiritual by the removal of sin, but this removal comes from attaining to the life of faith and following the teachings of God.

A Christian may come forward with counter-interpretations to every verse a Bahá'í may cite. However, the Bahá'í view is thoroughly applicable to all of the Scriptures and is also affirmed by reason and science. No denial of the Scriptures is suggested, nor is there any failure to state the importance of the truths contained in Scripture.

Some Christians assert that the resurrection is proof of Jesus' deity because only God has power over death. In a different way, a Bahá'í interpretation of the resurrection also provides proof of Jesus' sovereignty over death, that is, the spiritual death of the soul. Jesus' spiritual effect on the lives of His followers and on the establishment of the Church is truly a sign of the efficacy of His love and testimony to His sovereignty, His power, His majesty and all the other spiritual qualities that characterize, and prove that He is a Manifestation of God.

The physical resurrection is not necessary to prove Jesus' deity or divinity, nor is it necessary to prove that He has the power to impart eternal life. It is not unique among the world's religions in believing that God has power over all things, including the power to secure eternal life. So, belief in a physical resurrection is not needed to establish or to convince people of these truths.

**BIBLICAL REFERENCES FOR PART FOUR**
The following verses can be used to construct an outline in our Bibles for future reference:

Jesus Came Down From Heaven (*Some Answered Questions* 119-20)
   John 3:13
   John 6:38, 41-2

The Risen Body of Christ is the Church:
    Rom. 12:5 'one body in Christ'
    1 Cor. 12:12-13 'baptized into one body'
    1 Cor. 12:25 'no schism in the body'
    1 Cor. 12:27 'you are the body of Christ'
    Col. 1:18 'He is the head of the body'
    Eph. 2:5-6 'members of His body, and His flesh'
The Spiritual Resurrection:
    1 Cor. 15:42-4 'it is raised in a spiritual body'
    1 Cor. 15:50 'flesh and blood cannot inherit
      the kingdom'

## SUGGESTED BOOKS FOR FURTHER READING

The following books may be of interest to Bahá'ís who wish to pursue a more scholarly study of the contemporary views and controversies concerning the resurrection narratives.

There are a number of Christian scholars who have examined the resurrection accounts and draw conclusions that support, and are similar in some regards to, the Bahá'í understanding. *The Resurrection and Modern Biblical Thought*, edited by Paul De Surgy, gives an overview of such scholarship.

Another book that is of interest is *The Formation of the Resurrection Narratives* by Reginald H. Fuller. Fuller suggests that the differences in the accounts are vehicles for expressing specific theological ideas intended by the authors of the Gospel. For a typical overview of modern conservative Christian reasoning about the resurrection see Josh McDowell's *The Resurrection Factor*. This is a book for the general reader which attempts to prove that the resurrection is literal.

The resurrection is a subject that often sparks debate among Christians. Some Christians accept the view that modern biblical research has disproved the authenticity of the

Gospel's accounts of the post-resurrection appearances of Christ, thus suggesting that belief in the physical resurrection is a view that developed later. Conservative Christians will almost always reject such views. The following is an example of the type of detail such debates involve: The last part of the Gospel of Mark, for instance, (16:9-20) which describes the appearance of the resurrected Christ, according to some scholars, shows stylistic differences that suggest that it was not written by the same person who wrote the preceding text. Furthermore, some of the oldest surviving texts, the *Codex Sinaiticus* and the *Codex Vaticanus*, do not contain the verses in question: 9 to 20. For this reason, some scholars argue that they are later additions and should not be accepted. However, we should consider whether these last verses were lost from an account and rewritten on the basis of other early authentic accounts. Also, are these accounts theologically sound and a consistent use of spiritual symbol?

In *The Resurrection Narratives: A Redactional Study*, Grant R. Osborne examines the narratives using modern methods of biblical scholarship to defend the traditional and even literal understanding of the resurrection. Obviously, scholars are far from reaching agreement on these matters.

In the next chapter we will examine some specific ways in which the subject of Christian doctrines can be approached in dialogues between Bahá'ís and Christians.

*part five*

CONCLUSION

# 13

## CONCLUSION

**PRACTICAL SUGGESTIONS ON THE ART OF DIALOGUE**
The following are a series of hypothetical dialogues between a
Bahá'í and a Christian that illustrate how conversations
about Christian doctrines can be conducted. These are only
very general examples and do not represent attempts to
explore fully any one particular issue or series of issues. The
objective of these dialogues is merely to show how a Bahá'í
might seek to fulfil certain Bahá'í goals, that is, to speak in a
respectful manner, to convey the Bahá'í acceptance of the
Bible and Christ, to avoid hair-splitting, and ultimately to
direct the conversation to the truth of Bahá'u'lláh:
humankind's hope for this age.

**DIALOGUE ONE**
The first dialogue presents a very broad conversation about a
variety of doctrinal issues. The following dialogues show how
discussions about the authority of the Bible, the deity of
Christ, the Atonement, and the Resurrection might be
conducted.

> **Christian:** You say you are a Bahá'í. If it contradicts
> the Bible, there is no way I would accept it.
>
> **Bahá'í:** People interpret the Bible differently.
> Nevertheless, the Bahá'í Faith regards the Bible as the
> Word of God. Bahá'u'lláh says, 'Reflect: the words of

the verses themselves eloquently testify to the truth that they are of God' [*Certitude* 84].

**Christian:** If you accept the Bible then you must recognize that Jesus Christ is the Son of God.

**Bahá'í:** Bahá'u'lláh says, 'Say, this is the One Who hath glorified the Son and hath exalted His Cause' [*Tablets of Bahá'u'lláh* 12].

**Christian:** But do you believe that Jesus is God?

**Bahá'í:** Bahá'u'lláh says that those who failed to accept Christ deprived themselves of 'beholding the face of God' [*Certitude* 18].

**Christian:** But do you believe that Jesus died for your sins?

**Bahá'í:** Bahá'u'lláh says that Jesus Christ sacrificed Himself 'as a ransom for the sins and iniquities of all the peoples of the earth' [*Gleanings* 75-6].

**Christian:** What about the Resurrection? Do you believe that Jesus rose from the dead?

**Bahá'í:** People differ in their understanding of the Resurrection. Nevertheless, Bahá'u'lláh's son, 'Abdu'l-Bahá, teaches that the resurrection is a spiritual fact. The resurrection is an important subject. As you are no doubt aware, Paul says, 'if Christ is not risen, then our preaching is vain and your faith is also vain' [1 Cor. 15:14]. 'Abdu'l-Bahá said Paul was like 'a divine philosopher' [Balyuzi,

'Abdu'l-Bahá 354] who was in 'close embrace with' Christ [Tablets of 'Abdu'l-Bahá Abbas 740].

**Christian:** If you accept Jesus Christ why do you need to accept Bahá'u'lláh? Christ said, 'I am the way, the truth, and the life. No one comes to the Father except through Me' [John 14:6].

**Bahá'í:** What you say is true. Moreover, 'Abdu'l-Bahá said, Christ sat upon 'a heavenly throne', an 'Eternal Throne from which' He 'reigns for ever', and that 'His Kingdom is everlasting'. The reality of Christ, He said 'is ever-living, everlasting, eternal' [Promulgation 395]. I believe Bahá'u'lláh and Christ are one. I accept Bahá'u'lláh because He manifests God. Who am I to reject God's Messenger? After all, even the appearance of Christ did not negate the truth of Moses. The evidences of Bahá'u'lláh are so great that no one who is informed of them can possibly deny that they are from God. Would you like to know more about the life and teachings of Bahá'u'lláh?

This dialogue illustrates the positive advantage of emphasizing areas of agreement to avoid conflict and lead up to a discussion of the truth of Bahá'u'lláh.

Now, suppose that the Christian had insisted on discovering some difference of understanding of the Bible. In many cases such an enquiry is sparked by sincere interest, but sometimes such insistence has the objective of trying to engage the Bahá'í in hair-splitting, the unprofitable dispute of fine points of doctrine in an attempt to prove the Bahá'í to be in error. Christianity has been marred by a long history of such disputes among its own adherents, and many

of these disputes have remained unresolved to this day.
Even if we are well informed in Christian theology, we are
unlikely to resolve such controversies without the Christian
first accepting the authority of Bahá'u'lláh. Our goal is to
teach the message of Bahá'u'lláh, and it is therefore best if
we can master the art of avoiding needless conflicts and
sources of contention. Such adversarial conversations rarely
lead to a discovery of the truth.

The following two dialogues illustrate how a more
confrontational situation might be handled. The first
dialogue involves the incarnation and the second the
resurrection. The Christian reflects a traditional conservative
understanding.

## DIALOGUE TWO
In this first situation the Bahá'í knows very little about the
Bible apart from the fact that the Bahá'í sacred texts affirm
the Bible's inspiration.

> **Christian:** You say the Bible is the word of God and
> that Bahá'u'lláh recognizes the Sonship of Jesus
> Christ. But do you recognize that Jesus is God made
> flesh, God incarnate?

> **Bahá'í:** I know that the Bahá'í Faith accepts the
> Bible, but I am not versed in the Christian
> interpretation of the Scriptures, nor have I had time,
> as yet, to give them the attention they deserve.
> Could you show me where in the Bible it is taught
> that Jesus is God incarnate?

> **Christian:** Yes. In the Gospel of John it says that the
> Word was with God, the Word was God, and the
> Word became flesh in the Person of Jesus Christ.

**Bahá'í:** How is it that this means God became flesh - incarnate - as you say?

**Christian:** The words 'became flesh' in Latin are 'in carne', which is where the word incarnation came from. Incarnation means God became flesh.

**Bahá'í:** Could it not be understood in another way?

**Christian:** How?

**Bahá'í:** To mean that the attributes of God became manifested in the historical person Jesus Christ who, like us, possessed a physical body, that is, flesh. Consider this analogy using a sun and a mirror. The physical person Jesus is like a mirror reflecting the light of God. In this way, God is manifest in the world through the Person of Christ, - in the flesh, so to speak.

**Christian:** I accept the traditional interpretation.

**Bahá'í:** I respect your beliefs and I'm happy that we both accept the Bible even though we may understand it differently. Christ came into the world to impart eternal life to all who believe in Him. I accept and believe in Christ. It would not do justice to the greatness of Jesus' teachings if people prevented themselves from respecting one another owing to differences of interpretation over the Scriptures that He inspired.

**Christian:** I can agree with that.

**Bahá'í:** Bahá'u'lláh affirms the truth of Christ and

the Bible. Would you like to hear more about the teachings and life of Bahá'u'lláh?

**DIALOGUE THREE**
In this dialogue, the Bahá'í has some knowledge of the Bible. Once again, the Christian reflects a traditional conservative understanding.

**Christian:** You say that the Bahá'í Faith accepts the Bible. Do you therefore accept that Jesus Christ rose bodily and physically from the dead?

**Bahá'í:** We accept the truth of the Bible.

**Christian:** Well then, you must therefore accept the bodily resurrection of Christ.

**Bahá'í:** I accept that the resurrection is an important spiritual fact.

**Christian:** The Bible teaches that it is a material fact!

**Bahá'í:** We both accept the resurrection, but understand it differently. Why is it important for people to believe that the Bible should be interpreted literally so that the resurrection becomes a physical and material matter?

**Christian:** Because it proves that Christ is sovereign Lord. That is, He has power over death. This proves that when He returns He has power to raise the dead and give them eternal life.

**Bahá'í:** I accept what you say as truth, that is, that

Christ is sovereign Lord and has the power to raise people from the dead. So, we agree, the resurrection is true, important, and it has the same ultimate significance to both of us.

**Christian:**  So you believe in the physical resurrection?

**Bahá'í:**  I believe the resurrection to be an important spiritual fact, and that Jesus is Lord and has the power to give us eternal life. The important points we agree on. It is important to me that I don't give you the mistaken impression that the Bahá'í Faith fails to accept the eternal truth and testimony of the Bible. However, by 'dead' I understand 'spiritually dead'.

**Christian:** Could you explain more?

**Bahá'í:** Christ said to one of His disciples who had asked if he could first go and bury His father before following Christ, let the dead bury the dead. It is clear that Christ meant, let the spiritually dead - in this context - bury the physically dead. Christ wished to emphasize that turning to God was more important that anything else, so He likened spiritual death to physical death. Jesus' sovereignty over death refers to His power to impart to you spiritual life. The Scriptures are not concerned with the things of this world. Paul explains the resurrection in 1 Corinthians, chapter 15, and in that same chapter, verse 50, says 'flesh and blood cannot inherit the kingdom of God'.

**Christian:** Are you saying that Christ could not conquer physical death?

**Bahá'í:** I only want to understand what Christ meant by His teachings, not to determine whether Christ could or could not work physical miracles. God has power to do whatsoever He wishes. My concern is simply to understand what was actually meant in the Gospel by resurrection. People interpret things differently, what is important is that we seek the truth in a spirit worthy of Christ's example of compassion and tolerance.

**Christian:** We clearly interpret things differently.

**Bahá'í:** That is true. People frequently differ in their interpretations of Scripture. Nevertheless, Bahá'u'lláh affirms the truth of Christ and the Bible. Would you like to hear more about the life and teachings of Bahá'u'lláh?

These dialogue examples are not provided as a way of showing the only possible or correct answers. Different situations obviously have different requirements. They are simply given in order to show a few ways of approaching topics by emphasizing areas of agreement in constructive dialogues, and avoiding unnecessary disputes. When a dialogue is concluded, it is far preferable if the Christian remembers the Bahá'í as one who professed a Faith that affirmed and respected Christ and the Bible and moreover, showed respect for Christians as well. If we allow ourselves to be drawn into heated discussions over Christian doctrines, even if we provide all the correct answers, we may only be remembered as believers of a religion that holds to views they do not accept.

It should be noted that in these dialogues the Bahá'í is not concerned with making any assertion that the Christian's views are in error. People can come to discover what is in error for themselves after they have been given an alternative interpretation. The example of Bahá'u'lláh illustrates this approach:

> it is said: 'Fasting is illumination, prayer is light.' One day, a well-known divine came to visit Us. While We were conversing with him, he referred to the above-quoted tradition. He said: 'Inasmuch as fasting causeth the heat of the body to increase, it hath therefore been likened unto the light of the sun; and as the prayer of the night-season refresheth man, it hath been compared unto the radiance of the moon.' Thereupon We realized that that poor man had not been favoured with a single drop of the ocean of true understanding, and had strayed far from the burning Bush of divine wisdom.[56] We then politely observed to him saying: 'The interpretation your honour hath given to this tradition is the one current amongst the people. Could it not be interpreted differently?' He asked Us: 'What could it be?' We made reply: 'Muhammad, the Seal of the Prophets, and the most distinguished of God's chosen Ones, hath likened the Dispensation of the Qur'án unto heaven, by reason of its loftiness, its paramount influence, its majesty, and the fact that it comprehendeth all religions. And as the sun and moon constitute the brightest and most prominent luminaries in the heavens, similarly in the heaven of the religion of God two shining orbs have been ordained - fasting and prayer. "Islam is heaven; fasting is its sun, prayer, its moon." ' (Certitude 39-40)

56. In this instance Bahá'u'lláh appears to be rejecting the religious leader's interpretation because it never goes beyond the material limitations of this world. Even though the Muslim divine has interpreted light as a symbol, he thinks that it points to another material phenomenon, in this case, the material heat of the body, supposedly arising from the act of fasting. Hence, the interpretation fails to discover the purpose of the verse, which is to provide spiritual guidance for the soul.

Notice that Bahá'u'lláh does not tell the Muslim divine that he is in error, nor does He openly reject his interpretation. He simply acknowledges the general acceptance of the view and then politely asks the Muslim if he would be interested in hearing an alternative view. The two phrases, 'The interpretation your honour hath given to this tradition is the one current amongst the people. Could it not be interpreted differently?' illustrate a beautiful and respectful way of approaching doctrinal issues and conflicting interpretations of the Scriptures. When we are presented with the literal interpretation of the Resurrection, the doctrine of Original Sin, and so on, we can simply acknowledge that it is the interpretation or understanding traditionally accepted, and then politely ask: 'Could it not be interpreted differently?'

## THE IMPORTANCE OF ESTABLISHING A SPIRIT OF FRIENDLINESS

In the first pages of this book we discussed the importance of Bahá'u'lláh's teaching: 'Consort with the followers of all religions in a spirit of friendliness and fellowship' (*Tablets of Bahá'u'lláh* 22). In both Volumes 1 and 2 of *Preparing for a Bahá'í/Christian Dialogue*, we have focused on the emphasis of legitimate and important areas of agreement with Christians as a means for establishing this fellowship.

With regard to the Gospel we have emphasized our acceptance of its 'divine inspiration' (*Promised Day* 109). With regard to Christ, we have emphasized our acceptance of His 'Sonship and Divinity' (ibid. 109). Concerning atonement, we have emphasized how Christ gave His life 'as a ransom for the sins and iniquities of all the people of the earth' (*Gleanings* 76), and how, through His sacrifice, 'a fresh capacity was infused into all created things' (ibid. 85). With regard to the Resurrection, we have emphasized that it is 'a spiritual and divine fact' (*Some Answered Questions* 120).

Emphasizing these areas of obvious agreement between Christianity and the Bahá'í Faith is one of the best ways we can lay a strong foundation of fellowship. Within the context of this fellowship we have the opportunity for positive and constructive discussions with Christians about the evidences of Bahá'u'lláh, His teachings, the fulfilment of prophecy and many other issues. Whatever the doctrine or issue, this foundation of fellowship is first established by pointing out the essential areas of agreement, after which other aspects of the truth can be explained. If antagonism arises we should always return to and re-emphasize the areas of agreement until the spirit of fellowship is restored.

To persist in the explanation of a point of disagreement while antagonism exists only adds fuel to the fire. It is preferable to stop and let that person say all that he or she has to say. Then re-affirm the areas of agreement. If no receptivity or goodwill is perceived, then, as Bahá'u'lláh instructs us, 'leave him unto himself, and beseech God to guide him' (Gleanings 289). Bahá'u'lláh writes:

That the divers communions of the earth, and the manifold systems of religious belief, should never be allowed to foster the feelings of animosity among men, is, in this Day, of the essence of the Faith of God and His Religion. (Epistle 13)

# ABBREVIATIONS

## THE OLD TESTAMENT

| | |
|---|---|
| Genesis | Gen. |
| Exodus | Exod. |
| Leviticus | Lev. |
| Numbers | Num. |
| Deuteronomy | Deut. |
| Joshua | Jos. |
| Judges | Jud. |
| Ruth | Ruth |
| 1 Samuel | 1 Sam. |
| 2 Samuel | 2 Sam. |
| 1 Kings | 1 Kings |
| 2 Kings | 2 Kings |
| 1 Chronicles | 1 Chron. |
| 2 Chronicles | 2 Chron. |
| Ezra | Ezra |
| Nehemiah | Neh. |
| Esther | Esther |
| Job | Job |
| Psalms | Ps. |
| Proverbs | Pro. |
| Ecclesiastes | Eccles. |
| Song of Solomon | Song of Sol. |
| Isaiah | Isa. |
| Jeremiah | Jer. |
| Lamentations | Lam. |
| Ezekiel | Ezek. |
| Daniel | Dan. |
| Hosea | Hosea |
| Joel | Joel |
| Amos | Amos |
| Obadiah | Obad. |
| Jonah | Jonah |
| Micah | Micah |
| Nahum | Nah. |
| Habakkuk | Hab. |
| Zephaniah | Zeph. |
| Haggai | Hag. |
| Zechariah | Zech. |
| Malachi | Mal. |

## THE NEW TESTAMENT

| | |
|---|---|
| Matthew | Matt. |
| Mark | Mark |
| Luke | Luke |
| John | John |
| The Acts | Acts |
| Romans | Rom. |
| 1 Corinthians | 1 Cor. |
| 2 Corinthians | 2 Cor. |
| Galatians | Gal. |
| Ephesians | Eph. |
| Philippians | Philip. |
| Colossians | Col. |
| 1 Thessalonians | 1 Thess. |
| 2 Thessalonians | 2 Thess. |
| 1 Timothy | 1 Tim. |
| 2 Timothy | 2 Tim. |
| Titus | Titus |
| Philemon | Phil. |
| Hebrews | Heb. |
| James | James |
| 1 Peter | 1 Pet. |
| 2 Peter | 2 Pet. |
| 1 John | 1 John |
| 2 John | 2 John |
| 3 John | 3 John |
| Jude | Jude |
| Revelation | Rev. |

## BIBLES

| | |
|---|---|
| American Standard Version | ASV |
| King James Version | KJV |
| The Modern Language Bible | ML |
| New International Version | NIV |
| New King James Version | NKJV |
| Revised Standard Version | RSV |

# BIBLIOGRAPHY

'Abdu'l-Bahá. *Paris Talks. Addresses given by 'Abdu'l-Bahá in Paris in 1911-1912*. London: Bahá'í Publishing Trust, 11th ed., 1969.

— *The Promulgation of Universal Peace: Talks Delivered by 'Abdu'l-Bahá During His Visit to the United States and Canada in 1912*. Comp. Howard MacNutt. Wilmette, Ill.: Bahá'í Publishing Trust, 1982 ed.

— *The Secret of Divine Civilization*. Trans. Marzieh Gail and Ali Kuli Khan. Wilmette, Ill.: Bahá'í Publishing Trust, 3rd ed, 1975.

— *Selections from the Writings of 'Abdu'l-Bahá*. Comp. Research Department of the Universal House of Justice, trans. Marzieh Gail and a Committee at the Bahá'í World Centre. Haifa, Israel: Bahá'í World Centre, 1982.

— *Some Answered Questions*. Comp. and trans. Laura Clifford Barney. London: Kegan Paul, Trench, Trubner and Co. Ltd., 1908. Rev. ed. London: Bahá'í Publishing Trust, 1964.

— *Tablets of Abdul-Baha Abbas*. New York: Bahá'í Publishing Committee, 1909-16, 1930.

Aldwinkle, Russell F. *Jesus - A Savior or The Savior?* Macon, Georgia: Mercer University Press, 1982.

Arcer, L. Gleason. *Encyclopedia of Bible Difficulties.* Grand Rapids, Mich.: Zondervan Publishing House, 1982.

Báb, The. *Selections from the Writings of The Báb.* Comp. by the Research Department of the Universal House of Justice, trans. Habib Taherzadeh and a Committee at the Bahá'í World Centre. Haifa, Israel: Bahá'í World Centre, 1976.

*Bahá'í Prayers: A Selection of Prayers Revealed by Bahá'u'lláh, The Báb, and 'Abdu'l-Bahá.* Wilmette, Ill.: Bahá'í Publishing Trust, 1954, 1982.

*Bahá'í World Faith: Selected Writings of Bahá'u'lláh and 'Abdu'l-Bahá.* Comp. Horace Holley. Wilmette, Ill.: Bahá'í Publishing Committee, 1943.

Bahá'u'lláh. *Epistle to the Son of the Wolf.* Trans. Shoghi Effendi. Wilmette, Ill.: Bahá'í Publishing Trust, 1941, 3rd rev. ed., 1976.

— *Gleanings from the Writings of Bahá'u'lláh.* Trans. Shoghi Effendi. Wilmette, Ill.: Bahá'í Publishing Trust, 1939, 2nd ed., 1956.

— *The Kitáb-i-Iqán (The Book of Certitude).* Trans. Shoghi Effendi. Wilmette, Ill.: Bahá'í Publishing Trust, 1931, 3rd ed., 1974.

— *Prayers and Meditations of Bahá'u'lláh.* Trans. Shoghi Effendi. Wilmette, Ill.: Bahá'í Publishing Trust, 1938, 1972.

— *Synopsis and Codification of the Laws and Ordinances of the Kitáb-i-Aqdas.* Trans. Shoghi Effendi. England: Broadwater Press Limited, 1973.

— *Tablets of Bahá'u'lláh revealed after the Kitáb-i-Aqdas*. Comp. Research Department of the Universal House of Justice. Trans. by Habib Taherzadeh and a Committee at the Bahá'í World Centre. Haifa, Israel: Bahá'í World Centre, 1978.

Balyuzi, H.M. *'Abdu'l-Bahá*. Oxford: George Ronald, 1972.

Barackman, Floyd H. *Practical Christian Theology*. Old Tappan, N.J.: Fleming H. Revell Co., 1984.

Beasley-Murray, G.R. *Jesus and the Future*. London: Macmillan, 1954.

Berkhof, Louis. *A History of Christian Doctrines*. Grand Rapids, Mich.: Baker Book House, 1937, 8th imp., 1986.

*Bhagavad-Gita: As It Is*. Trans. and Compiled. by A.C. Bhaktivedanta Swami Prabhapada, New York: Collier Books, 1972.

*The Holy Bible, New King James Version*. Nashville Tenn.: Thomas Nelson Inc., 1982.

Buchanan, E.S. *The Records Unrolled*. London: John Ouseley Limited, no date.

Dampier, Sir William. *A History of Science and its Relation with Philosophy and Religion*. New York: Macmillan, 1936.

Dillistone, F. W. *The Christian Understanding of Atonement*. SCM Press, 1982.

Finegan, Jack. *Encountering New Testament Manuscripts*. Grand Rapids, Mich.: William B. Eerdmans Publishing Co., 1974.

Frye, Roland M., ed. *Is God a Creationist?* New York: Charles Scribner's Sons Publishers, 1983.

Fuller, Reginald H. *The Formation of the Resurrection Narratives.* New York: Macmillan, 1971.

Geisler, Norman L. *A General Introduction to the Bible.* Chicago, Ill.: Moody Press, 1982.

Halley, Henry H. *Halley's Bible Handbook.* Grand Rapids, Mich.: Zondervan Publishing House, 24th edn, 1965.

Henry, Carl F.H., ed. *Basic Christian Doctrines.* Grand Rapids, Mich.: Baker Book House, 1962, 8th imp., 1985.

Hick, John and Brian Hebblethwaite. *Christianity and Other Religions: Selected Readings.* Philadelphia: Fortress Press, 1980.

Hoover, Arlie J. *Fallacies of Evolution.* Grand Rapids, Mich.: Baker Book House, 1977.

Hordern, William E. *A Layman's Guide to Protestant Theology.* New York: Macmillan, 1978.

*The Individual and Teaching.* Wilmette, Illinois: Bahá'í Publishing Trust, 1977.

Kenyon, Sir Frederic. *Our Bible and the Ancient Manuscripts.* New York: Harper and Row, 1962.

*Lights of Guidance, A Bahá'í Reference File.* Compiled by Helen Hornby. New Delhi, India: Bahá'í Publishing Trust, 1st edn, 1983.

Lindsell, Harold, *The Battle for the Bible*, Grand Rapids, Mich., Zondervan Publishing House, 1976.

*The Bible in the Balance*. Grand Rapids, Mich.: Zondervan Publishing House, 1979.

Lindsey, Hal. *The Late Great Planet Earth*. Grand Rapids, Mich.: Zondervan Publishing House, 1970.

Marsden, George. *Evangelicalism and Modern America*. Grand Rapids, Mich.: Eerdmans, 1984.

— *Fundamentalism and American Culture*. Oxford: Oxford University Press, 1982

McDowell, Josh. *The Resurrection Factor*. San Bernardino, Calif.: Here's Life Publishers, 1981.

McDowell, Josh and Don Stewart. *Answers to Tough Questions*. San Bernardino, Calif.: Here's Life Publishers, 1980.

— *Understanding Non-Christian Religions*, San Bernardino, Calif.: Here's Life Publishers, 1982.

Osborne, Grant R. *The Resurrection Narratives: A Redactional Study*. Grand Rapids, Mich.: Baker Book House, 1984.

Parrinder, Geoffrey. *Avatar and Incarnation*. New York: Oxford University Press, 1982.

— *Jesus in the Qur'án*. New York: Oxford University Press, 1977.

Roberts, The Rev. Alexander, and James Donaldson, ed. *The Anti-Nicene Fathers, vol. VII*. Grand Rapids, Mich.: Eerdmans, 1979.

Rogers, Jack B., and Donald K. McKim. *The Authority and Interpretation of the Bible*. San Francisco, Calif.: Harper and Row, 1979.

*Sacred Books of the Buddhist, Vol. 3, 'Dialogues of the Buddha'*. Trans. by T.W. and C.A.F. Rhys Davies, London: Luzac and Company, 5th edn, 1971.

*Scientific Creationism*, (Public School Edn). Prepared by the Institute for Creation Research and edited by Henry Morris. San Diego, Calif.: C.L.P. Publishers, 1981.

Shoghi Effendi. *God Passes By*. Wilmette, Ill.: Bahá'í Publishing Trust, 1974.

— *The Promised Day is Come*. Wilmette, Ill.: Bahá'í Publishing Trust, rev. edn., 1980.

— *The World Order of Bahá'u'lláh: Selected Letters from Shoghi Effendi*. Wilmette, Ill.: Bahá'í Publishing Trust, 2nd rev. ed., 1974.

Sours, Michael W. *Preparing for a Bahá'í/Christian Dialogue: Understanding Biblical Evidence, Volume One*. Oxford: Oneworld Publications, 1990.

Surgy, Saul De, ed. *The Resurrection and Modern Biblical Thought*. Trans. by Charles Underhill Quinn. New York: Corpus Books, 1970.

Vine, W.E. *Vine's Expository Dictionary of Biblical Words*. Nashville: Thomas Nelson, rev. edn., 1985.

# GENERAL INDEX

Abelard, Peter 124n
Adam 99, 103, 112, 124, 125,
    126, 127
'Abdu'l-Bahá
    explains
        atonement 22, 100,
            123, 124n, 126, 127
        fundamentals of
            Christ's teachings 69
        importance of faith
            116-18
        life after death 107, 115
        meaning of heaven
            138-9
        sacrifice of Jesus 123
        sin 111, 112
        spiritual life 113, 114
        why Apostles changed
            laws of Moses 46-7
        words of Paul 124-5
    extols Apostles of Christ
        42
    extols Paul 160, 161
    acknowledges atoning
        power of Jesus' death 22

'Abdu'l-Bahá (continued)
    affirms Bible 35, 36, 48, 49
    affirms spiritual truth of
        resurrection 135, 136-
        7ff, 160
    canon of Bible, and 35
    comments on Paul's
        writings 42n, 124-5
    concerning
        building friendships
            24-5
        equality of men and
            women 47
        Ishmael/Isaac
            discrepancy 56
    interprets New Testament
        42n
    refers to Jesus as the
        'Word' 38, 42, 94
    says Bible has been
        misinterpreted 52-4
    says Cause of Bahá'u'lláh
        is same as Christ's 63
    says Reality of Christ is
        everlasting and eternal

Bahá'u'lláh (continued)
  and women 47
  Temple of God 128
  writings of 129
Barackman, Floyd 30, 31, 33n,
  124n
Beasley-Murray 54n
Bhagavad-Gita 115n
Bible, (see also Pentateuch,
    Torah, Talmud, Gospel)
  'authentic Book' of God
    59
  authority of 29
  Bahá'ís encouraged to
    study 12-13
  Bahá'í Faith, supports 25
  canonicity of Books 34, 35
  Christian beliefs
    concerning 30ff
  errors in Bible, insig-
    nificant 38, 50, 54, 57
  'God-breathed' 36
  helps people find truth 25
  infallibility of 30, 31, 36,
    37, 38
  inerrancy of 30, 31, 42-5
  inspiration of 30, 31
  interpretation of 37, 38,
    52ff
  King James Version 33
  laws not suitable for this
    age 47
  literal interpretation of
    16, 17, 18
  additions unproven 53

Bible (continued)
  merits of 61
  misinterpreted 53, 54
  narratives of 39-41
  not only or last Book of
    God 65ff
  not wholly authentic 56,
    58ff
  one with Bahá'í Writings
    62-5
  Protestant emphasis on 29
  records unseemly sayings
    of unbelievers 40-1
  spiritual contents of 61
  terminology, as source of
    13
  transcription of 37, 38,
    52ff
  translation of 37, 38, 52ff
  verbal inspiration of 17n
  Word of God 21, 38
Book of Certitude (Kitáb-i-
    Iqán)
  calls Jesus 'Essence of the
    Spirit' 94
  concerning
    everlasting life 101
    faith and certitude 40
    forgiveness 106
    God's all-encompassing
      grace 68
    grace 104, 106, 118
    human potential to
      reflect attributes of
      God 78

# INDEX OF BIBLICAL REFERENCES

Romans (continued)
   6:15, p. 109, 129
   6:23, p. 99, 114
   7:23, p. 112
   8:5-6, p. 113
   8:13, p. 113
   8:14, p. 84, 95
   12:5, p. 139, 155
   14:14, p. 46
   15:19, p. 42
   16:17, p. 15

1 Corinthians
   1:18-24, p. 144
   12:12-13, p. 140, 155
   12:25, p. 140, 155
   12:27, p. 140, 155
   14:34-5, p. 47
   ch. 15, p. 150, 152
   15:6, p. 150
   15:14, p. 152, 160
   15:14-4, p. 153, 155
   15:22, p. 124
   15:50, p. 153, 155, 165

2 Corinthians
   3:6, p. 67, 70
   3:18, p. 82
   4:4, p. 82, 96
   5:21, p. 83

Galatians
   1:9, p. 62, 63, 64

Ephesians
   2:5, 6, p. 140, 155
   2:8, p. 115, 120
   2:9, p. 115
   5:29-30, p. 141, 147

Philippians
   2:5-6, p. 77

Colossians
   1:15, p. 77
   1:18, p. 140, 150
   2:9, p. 77
   2:15, p. 77

1 Timothy
   2:5, p. 96

2 Timothy
   3:16-17, p. 34-5, 65

Titus
   1:15, p. 46
   2:11, p. 68, 70, 120, 129

Hebrews
   4:12, p. 151
   9:22, p. 122
   11:17, p. 55

James
   1:15, p. 125
   2:21, p. 55
   2:26, p. 129

1 Peter
   3:15, p. 58

2 Peter
   3:15, p. 42

1 John
   1:5, p. 41
   3:1, p. 84, 95
   3:6, p. 109, 129
   4:9, p. 85
   4:12, p. 95